Nempnett Thi
Barrows, Names and Manors

Essays on the Landscape History of a
North Somerset Parish

Richard Dunn

NempnettBooks.co.uk

First published 2004
by NempnettBooks.co.uk
Email: info@nempnettbooks.co.uk

Typeset in Garamond by NempnettBooks.co.uk
Design by NempnettBooks.co.uk

Printed in Great Britain by Henry Ling Ltd, Dorset, DT1 1HD

ISBN 0-9548614-0-X

Contents

Acknowledgements

Many people have helped in the preparation of this book. I am grateful to Jane Dymock for the original suggestion which stimulated my interest in the history of the parish, and to Pete Hellier, Marguerite Lihou, John Malone, Jodie Lewis and Paul Cavill for their many helpful comments on various drafts. The staff at the Record Offices and Local Studies Libraries in Taunton Gloucester, Bristol and Exeter have been of great assistance; David Bromwich has been of especial help in this respect. Robert Dunning has provided invaluable assistance in translating and interpreting early documents, and Pauline Wheeler has also done some translation. Paul Cavill has been of great help in dealing with the complexities of place- and field-names, and Vera Baber has assisted in my researches into the Baber family. Bob Sydes, Peter Fowler and Vince Russett have provided many detailed insights into local archaeology.

The extracts of the Tithe Map used in figures 20, 45, 46, 47 and 56, and Plates 16 and 19, are reproduced courtesy of the Somerset Records Office. Figures 66 and 82 are published with the permission of Bristol Records Office. Figure 67 is copyright Alan Baber. Figures 71 and 72 are part of the Braikenridge Collection of the Somerset Archaeology and Natural History Society. Figures 31, 32, 33, 34 and 64 are copyright British Library. Figures 5, 13, 14 and 44 and the front cover use aerial photographs from the English Heritage National Monuments Record collection. Figure 35 is courtesy of Bristol Museum. All other figures and photographs are copyright of the author.

Preface

I moved to Nempnett Thrubwell in 1993, drawn by the sense of it being a place out-of-the-way and left behind by time. And of course that wonderful name. In fact the parish is as unusual as the name, quite different from its neighbours, with no central village but rather a scattering of houses along deeply-cut, winding lanes, a church far from the rest of the parish with just two farmhouses for company, and a landscape that has changed little for centuries and contains many traces of prehistory.

Although I always had a passing interest in the history of the place, other things took priority, until in 1999 I was asked by a friend to "pop down to the archives and find out a bit about the name". That marked the start of a period when for four or five years I gathered information, rather magpie-like, on all aspects of the parish and its history, visiting the Public Records Offices (the "archives"), reading various publications, discussing the area with local archaeologists, and searching the internet.

This book marks an outcome of that process. It has been written for anyone who is interested in finding out a bit more about Nempnett Thrubwell, especially its landscape, history and geography. I have tried to write in a way that assumes no knowledge of history or archaeology, and have used illustrations, maps and diagrams wherever possible. I was trained as a geographer, so I have a particular interest in where things are and where events took place (as well as when), hence the many maps. There is also quite a focus on the landscape: the patterns of fields, the development of settlement and the remnants of ancient landscapes such as barrows.

The title *Nempnett Thrubwell: Barrows, Names, and Manors* with its sub-title *Essays on the Landscape History of a North Somerset Parish* describe what the book is, and what it is not. This is not a "complete" local history of the parish; there is an emphasis on the landscape, with very little, for example, about the people and events of the 19th and 20th centuries, and on certain topics such as the church and chapel. Rather than order material strictly on the basis of when it happened I have grouped it together by themes, so that each chapter is designed as a "stand-alone" essay. Although the book is best read from front to back, the interested reader should be able to dip into a chapter that looks of special interest and find it relatively self-contained. (Readers interested in the 20th century history of the parish and more information about the church and chapel are directed to the parish millennium book *Nempnett Thrubwell: Times Remembered.*)

Most of this book is concerned with drawing together material already published or available in the archives, and a primary aim is to make this material more readily available to the general reader and to provide enough context to make it easily understood. In some places I have also speculated on the significance of evidence I have found, for example possible locations within the parish where there may be the remains of undiscovered archaeology. I hope these suggestions may of interest to those who might in the future have the time and inclination to look more deeply into the past of the parish.

List of Illustrations

1   Introduction

Nempnett Thrubwell is a small parish in northern Somerset located just north of the Mendips and about 13km south-west of Bristol - see Figure 1. The parish lies mostly on the southern slopes of the area of high ground known as Broadfield Down, Lulsgate Plateau or Felton Common, within the valley of the River Yeo. Much of the parish enjoys a south-facing aspect with fine views across the man-made Blagdon Lake to the Mendips beyond. However, these lovely views mean exposure to the prevailing south-westerlies, and strong winds are a common feature. The average annual rainfall is about 25cm.

A detailed map of the parish is shown in Figure 2. The parish is roughly triangular in shape, about 6km from north to south, and 3km from east to west, with an area of 7.3 sq kms (2.8 sq miles, 1800 acres). The southern boundary of the parish originally followed the course of the River Yeo, and 0.62 sq kms (153 acres) of the parish were "lost" when Blagdon Lake was completed in 1902. Early maps of the parish therefore extend down to the river. Not all the roads and lanes in the parish have names, but those that are generally known and used are shown. The most famous is the appropriately named Awkward Hill.

Historically the parish was in the County of Somerset, but it became part of the new County of Avon in 1974, and then in 1996 part of Bath and North East Somerset when Avon was reorganised.

Today there are about 60 dwellings in the parish, which are widely scattered with no real clustering in a central "village." The Church, dedicated to St. Mary, lies in an isolated position in the extreme east of the parish, with just one farm and one house nearby – see Plates 2 and 3. There is a group of dwellings strung along Nempnett Street, some 700m to the west, with a second and somewhat smaller cluster in West Town, a further 700m west - see Plates 4 and 5. There are other farms and houses scattered throughout the remainder of the parish, some in small clusters, some completely isolated.

This pattern of settlement is very unusual for this part of the country. Most of the nearby parishes have a main village, with a cluster of old houses around the church, to which have been added over the years various newer developments; this main centre is usually also the focus of the local network of roads, lanes, and footpaths in the parish. For example, Blagdon, Ubley, and Butcombe, take this form, while Winford Parish has a main village plus outlying smaller settlements of Felton and Regil. But in Nempnett Thrubwell there is no main village, no central cluster of houses, no obvious place where the visitor can stop and feel "in the middle of Nempnett," rather the parish is a place of winding lanes and scattered houses.

Current opinion suggests that this type of dispersed pattern of settlement is much older and more "normal" than the villages we tend to think of as characteristic of the English countryside.[1] To explain why Nempnett has such a distinct pattern of settlement is one of the aims of this book, although the question is complex and opinion is divided about the reasons behind the development of villages.

There have been some small but significant boundary changes in the parish over the past 160 years which are summarised in Figure 3. In 1841, the earliest date for which detailed maps and information are available, Butcombe Mill (a plot of 0.6 acres) was an outlying part of Nempnett Parish, that is to say it was legally part of the parish and paid its tithes to Nempnett Church. Similarly, a number of fields on the eastern edge of the parish, around Strode Farm, were "outlying islands" entirely surrounded by Winford parish. On the other side of the coin about 29 acres of land around Henmarsh Farm were at that time an outlying part of Winford Parish.

A series of Local Government Orders in the 1880's under the provisions of the "Divided Parishes Act" rearranged these areas to form parishes that had no outlying areas. In 1888 this boundary was recorded on the first edition of the Ordinance Survey maps, so this boundary is referred to here as "the 1888 boundary." This remained the legal extent of the parish until 1983 when about 120

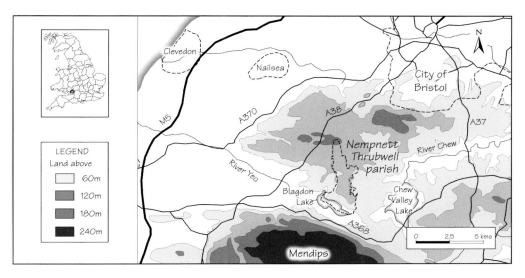

Figure 1: The regional setting of Nempnett Thrubwell

acres of land around Dewdown were transferred from Winford to Nempnett. This book will focus on the parish as defined by the 1888 boundary.

The question "when did the parish come into existence?" is frequently asked, but it is difficult if not impossible to answer. It is often written that parishes came into existence with the establishment of Christianity, roughly 700-900AD. However many archaeologists and historians are now suggesting that parish boundaries may date back even further, and that the ecclesiastical parishes may be based on land-use units of Roman or prehistoric times. These theories will be discussed at further length in later chapters.

The topography and geology of the parish are shown in Plate 1. The highest point in the parish is in the extreme north on the edge of Felton Common, at about 185m above sea level. The northern two thirds of the parish form an undulating plateau, mostly between 175 and 130m, that slopes gently southwards. The southern third of the parish is characterised by very steep slopes where the land drops from *c.* 130m to 50m towards Blagdon Lake. The soil is mainly heavy clay.

In terms of geology, the oldest rocks are the 345 million-year-old Carboniferous Limestones (d2 and d3 on Plate 1), which occur in the north of the parish and are part of the Broadfield Down high ground, although within the parish in most places

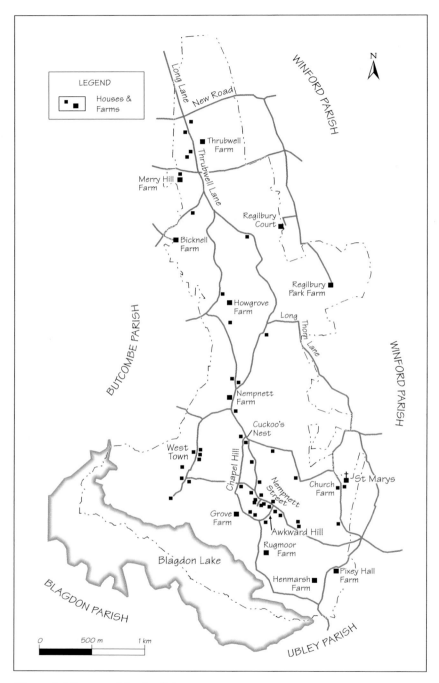

Figure 2: Nempnett Thrubwell 2001

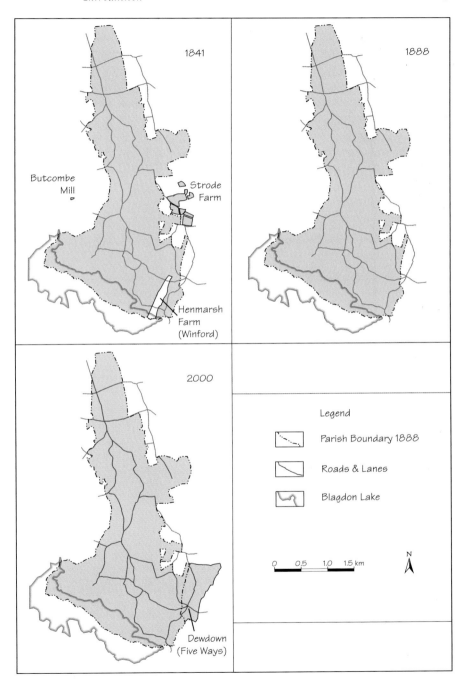

Figure 3: Boundary changes 1841-2000

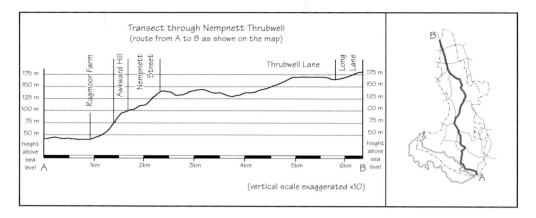

Figure 4: A transect of a journey through Nempnett Thrubwell

they are overlain by newer rocks, a mixture of clay and lias (fg-g1a
in Plate 1). Next in terms of age is the red Keuper Marl of the
Triassic period (f6), deposited 225 million years ago. In places this
marl is interspersed with the harder Butcombe Sandstone (BuS).
The youngest rocks are the Jurassic Lias series (195 million years
old), which overlie the Keuper Marl in places and form the higher
plateau land in the centre of the parish (g1 and g1a).

Another way of describing the topography of the parish is to
construct a transect of a journey showing the ups and downs of
the land. One such transect is shown in Figure 4, which traces
a journey from the south-east corner of the parish near Ubley
Mill (point A) to Long Lane in the north (point B). The first part
of the journey is along the flat land alongside Blagdon Lake, at
about 40m above sea level. Then, after passing Rugmoor Farm,
there is a very steep ascent, first up Awkward Hill and then, at
a lesser gradient, up Nempnett Street; over a distance of about
1.5kms the traveller climbs from 40m to 140m. The remainder
of the journey is across the gentle slopes of the high plateau, with
an overall ascent from 140m to 175m over a distance of about
4km.

If we wanted to sub-divide the parish into zones a natural
division is into three areas: the low, flattish land near the River
Yeo (much now under the lake), the steep slopes to the north,
and then the higher "plateau" of the northern part of the parish.
These different parts of the parish were for a long time a key
factor in determining how the land was used by those that settled
here.

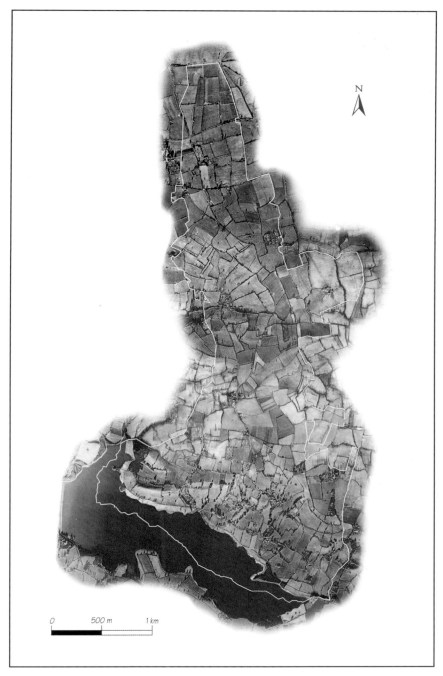

Figure 5: Aerial Photograph of Nempnett Thrubwell in 1946

The main features of the landscape today are the mosaic of mostly small, irregular fields predominantly given over to arable and pasture, the winding lanes, and the scattered houses. There is very little woodland; there are a few copses of trees, quite a few isolated established trees in the hedgerows, and some old trees stand alone in the middle of fields the only reminder of a long-ago removed hedge. An aerial photograph of the parish can give a "birds-eye" view of what this landscape is like and Figure 5 shows such an image for 1946.[2] The scale of Figure 5 is not ideal, as much of the detail is lost, but it serves to give an overview of the parish. More detailed parts of this image ("close-ups") are used later in the book (see Figures 13, 14, and 44) - see also the book front cover. The parish has changed relatively little since 1946, although there has been some limited removal of hedges and some established trees have been lost to the chainsaw or Dutch Elm disease.

The landscape of the parish is a rich historical document, having been formed by the actions of its inhabitants over the past thousands of years; the remaining chapters of this book discuss some of the rich and varied history that lies behind the current landscape.

2   Prehistoric and Roman Times

INTRODUCTION

The environment of the Yeo and Chew river valleys provided our predecessors with food and shelter in the early days of hunter-gathering, and then, as agriculture and industry developed, a productive and hospitable combination of soils, resources and climate. Thus, from what is currently known about the local area, is it likely that Nempnett Thrubwell was settled throughout the prehistoric and Roman periods. These very early times of human settlement, when the main preoccupation was simply to find enough to eat, hold a fascination for most of us. And there still remain within the landscape today some traces of these very first inhabitants of Nempnett.

Much of the detailed knowledge about local prehistoric and Roman life comes from two sets of nearby archaeological excavations, at Butcombe and Chew Valley Lake – see Figure 6. The excavations at Butcombe started in 1966 under the direction of Professor Peter Fowler, and the area includes a Roman villa at Lye Hole, Romano-British settlements at Scars Farm and Westmead, Romano-British field systems, and evidence of use at earlier dates. The majority of this work took place in Butcombe and Wrington parishes, but the Romano-British field systems extend eastwards into Nempnett so that many of the findings of this work are of particular interest.

The Chew Valley Lake archaeological excavations were carried out in 1953-55 prior to the creation of the lake, and these provide a second important local source. Following a preliminary evaluation of the whole area to be flooded, detailed studies were focused on seven areas: three large sites at Chew Park, Heriotts Bridge and Moreton, and four smaller sites at Stratford Mill, Ben Bridge, St. Cross Nunnery and Denny Moat – see Figure 6. The excavations at Chew Valley Lake, led by Professor Philip Rahtz, produced evidence for occupation throughout the prehistoric and Roman periods.

Another important nearby site is Pagans Hill (see Figure 6), which was excavated first between 1949 and 1953, and then in 1986, also under the direction of Professor Rahtz. The main findings are of a Roman temple complex, but there is also evidence of use throughout the prehistoric period.

As well as the archaeological evidence gained during excavations there are other ways in which the activities of prehistoric and Roman peoples remain as traces in today's landscape. The most obvious examples are physical monuments, such as the stone circles at Stanton Drew, the Iron Age hill forts at Burledge, Burrington, Cadbury, and Maes Knoll, and many Bronze Age and Iron Age barrows. There are less obvious physical examples too, such as the slight ridges in many fields of north Butcombe that, upon excavation in the mid-1970's, proved to be the remnants of Romano-British field boundaries.

Sometimes most or all of the physical evidence above ground has been removed, and only underground traces remain, so that excavation is necessary to determine the full nature of any archaeological remains. Traces or "echoes" of these underground remains may sometimes be detectable in aerial photography, since under favourable conditions buried remains may appear as crop or soil marks. For example, the outline of the Roman villa uncovered at Chew Park was visible from aerial photographs, and in the Butcombe study aerial photography was an important tool in the mapping of Romano-British field systems.

The traces of ancient peoples survive in other ways too. Strange twists and turns of parish boundaries may on occasion reflect the fact that when these boundaries were first laid out barrows were used as markers. And in an area where most fields are small and irregular the one dead-straight hedgerow, which runs on for some distance, may in fact mark the route of a long-lost Roman road. Traces may also survive through place- and field-names; all place- and field-names once had a clear and easily-understood meaning, but the passage of time has often made these original meanings obscure, and names with archaeological significance, for example references to now-destroyed barrows, may still remain.

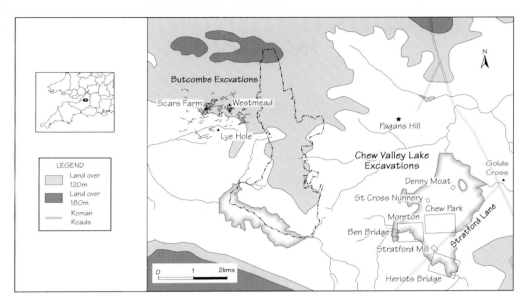

Figure 6: Selected archaeological sites in the Chew Valley and Wrington Vale

In the next sections of this chapter the nature of prehistoric and Roman life is discussed period by period, together with a summary of the known archaeological remains within the parish. Then there are two sections that discuss features that may possibly be traces of prehistoric activity. The possible significance of place- and field-names is discussed in Chapters 4 and 5. Hopefully these more speculative sections may be of help in focusing future archaeological work within the parish.

PALAEOLITHIC AND MESOLITHIC AGES (450,000-4,500BC)

The Palaeolithic saw great changes in the climate of southern England, including the advance and retreat of the ice caps and significant changes in sea levels. The most important characteristic of the Palaeolithic and Mesolithic ages, as far as the archaeological record is concerned, is that this was a period of hunter-gathering; the population depended upon the native flora and fauna, and was ignorant of agriculture, the domestication of animals, and the manufacture of pottery. Possessions would have been limited to stone tools and weapons, such as stone axes and flints, and some limited personal ornaments such as shell necklaces.

The nearest major excavated site of Palaeolithic date is at Burrington Coombe, where since 1797 a number of archaeologists have excavated the cave known locally as Aveline's Hole. The finds have included many human remains, numerous flints, stone knives, points, and scrapers, harpoons made from the antlers of red deer, and seashell necklaces. Analysis of the many animal bones found suggests a diet that included bear, red deer, reindeer, boar and wolf, as well as a number of small rodents, birds and fish, which would have been supplemented with wild vegetables and fruits collected by foraging.

At the Chew Valley Lake excavations a number of Palaeolithic stone implements were found, including a blade knife, untouched flint blades, flake knives and scrapers, some of which were comparable to the Upper Palaeolithic finds from Burrington Coombe. The only artefact definitely of Mesolithic type is a sandstone macehead found at Moreton. At Butcombe the possibility of Mesolithic activity is suggested by the occurrence of a flake of Portland Chert, a substance favoured by Neolithic populations throughout the South-West.

There are no known records from Palaeolithic or Mesolithic times within the parish of Nempnett Thrubwell, but, given that there have been no modern archaeological digs within the parish, this is perhaps not surprising. The evidence from excavations nearby suggests, however, that the parish was likely to have been a relatively desirable residential district even in those early eras.

NEOLITHIC AGE (4,500-2,300BC)

In the Neolithic period people learnt to domesticate animals and to grow grain, and communities based on agriculture became the norm. The Middle Neolithic is generally regarded as the first period when farming radically altered the countryside through widespread clearance of woodland. As the food supply became more regular, population densities increased, and with fixed settlements came real property and specialist knowledge such as pottery, weaving, and stone working. In our part of the country these peoples also built huge stone monuments, the long barrows, as some sort of ceremonial focus and memorial to their dead.

There is no doubt that there was widespread settlement at this time throughout the Yeo and Chew Valleys. Neolithic flint implements were found at almost all the sites examined at the Chew Valley Lake excavations; at Chew Park evidence of a small, round hut or house, about 3m in diameter, was found together with domestic refuse including flint and pottery. At Butcombe there were Neolithic finds of a stone axe fragment, flint flakes and a few implements; two probable post-holes suggested that structures of this period were once present. There is further evidence of Neolithic settlement at Winscombe, Camerton, Congresbury, and Burrington. There have been no archaeological excavations within Nempnett Thrubwell and thus there is no known direct evidence of Neolithic houses, farms or fields within the parish, but there is evidence of Neolithic burial.

Megalithic tombs and ceremonial structures are the most dramatic and visible evidence from the Neolithic era. The Stanton Drew stone circles are the best-known local example. Elsewhere through the region are a number of stone-built Neolithic long barrows, equally impressive in their own way, as they required many thousands of hours of effort to construct, and there are the remains of one such burial chamber in Nempnett at Fairy's Toot – see Figure 7.

Fairy's Toot is thought to have been built in the middle Neolithic as a collective grave; when intact it measured about 50m long by 25m wide and 5m high, and contained about a dozen stone chambers where the dead were interred. Sadly it was almost totally destroyed in the early 19th century, although there are some records, which include reports of finds of several skeletons and some animal bones. Exactly what function such a structure would have served in Neolithic times has been the subject of much debate, but it seems likely it would have served as both a central repository for the dead of a small community and as a centre for ceremonial activity. The full story of Fairy's Toot is told in Chapter 3.

Unfortunately, many barrows are known to have disappeared over the years, especially in the early 19th century when they were plundered for stone and then all traces cleared to increase the amount of productive land. Writing in the 1820s, John Skinner says that of five other nearby barrows of similar type to Fairy's Toot four have been "almost wholly removed" or "nearly obliterated from the face of the earth".[1] The present day record of features such as barrows is thus incomplete, and it is quite possible that other examples await discovery where the only remaining traces now are below ground or in place- or field-names.

The Neolithic is thus the earliest period for which we have definite evidence of people living in the parish. Fairy's Toot would have been an important ceremonial centre some five millennia ago. Although we are never likely to know the size of the population associated with it, or what area it served, it is clear that there must have been people here and in adjacent parishes. Further details of Neolithic settlement within the parish must await future archaeological work.

BRONZE AGE (2,300-700BC)

This period is characterised by bronze-working skills, the production of new tool types in flint and stone, and the adoption of new pottery styles; the early part of this age is the Beaker phase, named after a particular style of continental pottery. Burial ritual was based on round barrows, typically 10-20m in diameter and 1-2m high, and usually with a single central internment. These barrows are smaller and less substantial monuments than the Neolithic long barrows, and many have been almost levelled by the plough, destroyed during the Second World War, or removed for other reasons. In other cases without detailed investigation it is difficult to distinguish between round barrows and natural mounds of similar size or more recent features such as spoil heaps.

Evidence of Bronze Age occupation has been found at the Chew Park and Ben Bridge sites at the Chew Valley Lake excavations, dating to the early Bronze Age and Beaker periods. Finds included evidence of burial, numerous flint and stone artefacts, and many pottery shards. Of particular importance was a quern rubber, a stone device made of Pennant Sandstone for the hand milling of cereal into flour and meal, which implies local agriculture during the Beaker phase. Other nearby finds of note include a middle Bronze Age socketed axe at Lulsgate and a late Bronze Age socketed adze at Barrow Gurney, both now in the Bristol City Museum. There are no reported Bronze Age finds in Nempnett Thrubwell but there is evidence of Bronze Age burial.

The one site in Nempnett which has been classified with some certainty as Bronze Age is a barrow which lies some 400m to the west of Yeo House, at the end of a pronounced ridge overlooking Blagdon Lake, in the south-west of the parish, see

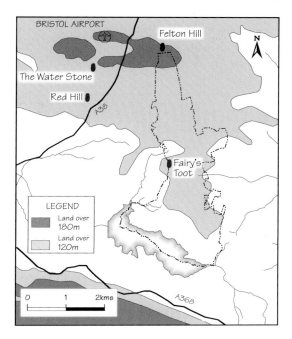

Figure 7: Long barrows in and near Nempnett Thrubwell

Figure 8 and Plate 6. This barrow has not been named in the literature, but is known as T292 in the widely-used University of Bristol Spelaeological Society (UBSS) scheme; here it will be referred to as Hawkridge Barrow, since the field in which it is located was known as Hawkridge at the time of the Tithe Map survey in the mid-19th century.

The barrow is reported in the 1938 edition of the UBSS journal, where is it described as "a small mound, 33ft [10m] in diameter and 3ft [0.9m] high". Leslie Grinsell, probably the foremost expert on Somerset barrows, visited Hawkridge Barrow on 27 September 1964, measured it as 11 paces [11m] in diameter and 3½ft [1.1m] high, and noted it was grass covered and that there were signs of a ditch. A visit in 1965 by G H Pitcher of the Ordnance Survey describes it thus: "This mound, 1.1m high, is situated at the western edge of a narrow ridge, at ST51236024. It is certainly artificial and is probably a bowl barrow".

The site is considered of sufficient importance to have been designated as a Scheduled Monument protected under Section I of the Ancient Monuments and Archaeological Areas Act of 1979. The schedule describes it as a bowl barrow, *c.* 1.2m high, 12m in diameter, surrounded by a ditch from which material was quarried during the construction of the monument. This ditch

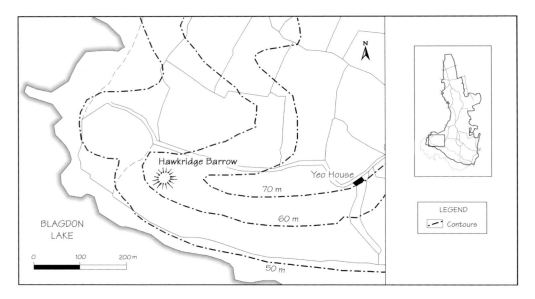

Figure 8: Hawkridge Barrow

has been largely in-filled over the years but survives as a buried feature *c.* 2m wide. In its original state a bowl barrow consists of a mound with a surrounding ditch; the mound covers a single burial, either inhumation or cremation, which is usually found in a cist, pit or urn below the centre of the mound, at or below the old turf level. It appears that no details of the internal structure of Hawkridge Barrow are known. There is a local tale that the burial was reused for burial in Victorian times, by some unwilling or unable to use St. Mary's graveyard. The barrow is on private land.

A second possible Bronze Age barrow has been identified in the north-west of the parish, adjacent to Butcombe Court - see Figure 9 and Plate 7. This was surveyed by E K Tratman of the UBSS in the 1920s, and given the UBSS number T36; it is described as "a simple bowl barrow measuring 72ft [22m] in diameter and 2½ft [0.8m] in height". Later investigations by Tratman and G H Pitcher, based in part on discussions with the Butcombe Court estate agent in 1965, note that "this is said to be a traditional burying place and as recently as 1905 a horse was buried in it".

When Leslie Grinsell visited this site in September 1964 he measured it as 24 paces [24m] in diameter and 2½ft [0.8m] in height

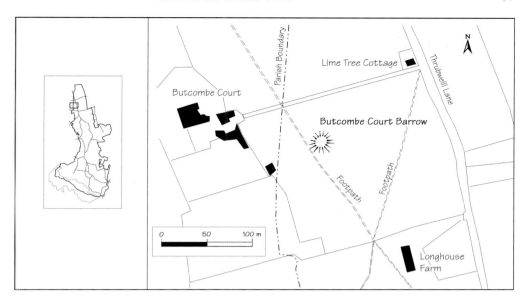

Figure 9: Butcombe Court Barrow

and noted that four firs were planted on it; he does not make any mention that he is doubtful of its authenticity. However, when Pitcher visited the site in 1965 he described it as 0.7m high and said "it is impossible to tell from the appearance of the mound whether it is completely modern or a re-utilised bowl barrow". The current state of opinion is that this is a possible bowl barrow, and it is recorded as such in the Sites and Monuments Record, but it does not have scheduled status. Further investigation would be necessary to determine its age. Of the four fir trees, just one remained in 2004. The barrow is on private land but footpaths run adjacent to it.

A third possible barrow in Nempnett was recorded by the 1920s UBSS fieldwork, located to the south of Merry Hill Farm in the north-west of the parish – see Figure 10. It was given the number T132 and measured 21ft [7m] across in one direction and 27ft [8m] in another, and was 1ft [0.3m] in height. When Grinsell visited the site in 1964 he described it as "doubtful." The Sites and Monuments Record now describes it as "an alleged barrow, but probably a modern spoil heap"; only a slight bank was apparent when E Dennsion visited the site in 1981 and the same is true today. The barrow is on private land, but is quite close to the lane.

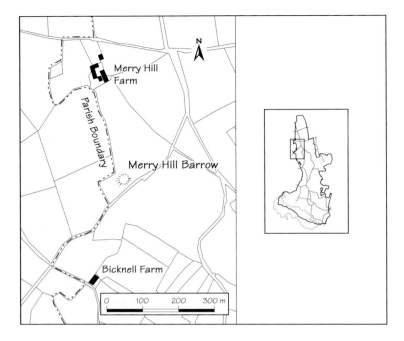

Figure 10: Merry Hill Barrow

In addition to these sites within the parish there are a number of barrows in adjacent parishes that lie extremely close to Nempnett, see Figure 11. The most notable is the cluster of three or four barrows on Felton Common in Winford parish, known locally as "The Mountains," which are only a few metres over the northern boundary of the parish. To the west is a barrow in Butcombe parish extremely close to the point where the parishes of Butcombe, Winford, and Nempnett meet. There are also reports of a barrow or barrows near Benches Lane in Winford, just north of Regilbury Court, very close to the parish boundary.

There are two theories as to why barrows are often found close to parish boundaries. The first is that when the boundaries were drawn up barrows were used as convenient markers, since they were something old, something people knew about, and something that was certainly not going to move. The second theory is more radical, namely that the barrows were actually built originally as boundary markers; barrows thus served to demarcate an area belonging to a certain tribe or family group, and may have played a mystical and protective role with the bones or spirits of the ancestors "guarding" the boundaries. The possible date-

The third phase of Roman occupation, from the late-third century onwards (*c.* 270-410AD), is a period of extensive villa building throughout rural areas of northern Somerset. The nearest known villas to Nempnett Thrubwell are at Lye Hole (Butcombe), Havyatt Green (near to where the A38 crosses the River Yeo), Chew Park (now under Chew Valley Lake), and Golds Cross (located just south of Knowle Hill at Double House Farm); and there are a series of further villas westwards along the valley of the Yeo River All these nearby villas date from this phase, as does the Roman temple at Pagans Hill. The late appearance of villas in the area compared to other parts of southern England has given rise to the theory that prior to *c.* 270AD the land was managed by "Imperial Estates" and was only sold off in the late third century either to boost the local economy or to provide new homes for wealthy landowners fleeing unrest in northern Gaul.

The main focus of the Butcombe excavations lies just to the north of the Lye Hole villa. At Westmead there is a rectangular building measuring 14m by 8m dated by coins to *c.* 270-345AD, part of which appears to have been used for keeping stock. Surrounding the building is a series of enclosures and small fields. About 600m to the west is another very similar settlement at Scars Farm – see Figure 6. The settlement appears to have been largely abandoned by the end of the fourth century.

Peter Fowler's overall assessment is that these settlements were "native farmsteads," with a generally low standard of living, which were probably tied economically and socially to the higher status villa at Lye Hole. Analysis of the animal remains at the native farmsteads suggests a mixed agricultural economy, with sheep, ox and a few pigs the main source of meat, but nearly all the choice cuts of meat were absent, suggesting these were sold or requisitioned, perhaps to the villa.

The Roman temple complex at Pagans Hill (see Figure 6) also dates to the late third century. The site, which is dedicated to an unknown cult, possibly worshipping the Roman god Mercury, is one of a number of pagan temples built in this period, typically on hilltop locations. The site includes an octagonal temple building, a ceremonial well, a priest's house, and guest wing, and there were a number of finds of exceptional quality; a sophisticated project like this is likely to signify that this was quite a prosperous area, with a Romanised elite of the villa owners using the temple for important ceremonial gatherings.

Much of Peter Fowler's work has concerned continuity in the landscape. A particularly striking example of this is Fowler's suggestion that the parish boundaries in the Wrington Vale may date back to Roman times. The argument runs as follows. The original laying out of Roman villas in the third century was a planned land division, designed to give a series of estates, which made efficient use of natural resources and shared them out equitably. In the Yeo Valley this meant estates that typically ran north-south and included a range of land, from low-lying meadow near the river, up the slopes to higher land that would have been suitable for ploughing, and the high pasture land of Broadfield Down or the Mendips.

Documentary evidence from the tenth century shows the Vale divided up into a series of Saxon estates of which "the existing parishes are, by and large, a fairly accurate reflection." And Fowler suggests that an apparent correlation between these estates and Roman villas implies that these Saxon estates reflected the older Roman land division. He notes that "if the basic trappings of the rural economy remain constant, whatever the political or tenurial arrangements, there should be no inherent improbability in the idea of a system which had been found to work at one time reappearing with different trappings in another".

It is an intriguing suggestion: that at one time Nempnett Thrubwell was a Roman estate, with a fine villa on the southern slopes overlooking the Yeo Valley and the Mendips, its occupants visiting the temple at Pagans Hill on feast days, and with the land around being cultivated by native farmsteads. Whether this is a fanciful tale or is something like the truth only time will tell.

There are, however, two definite pieces of evidence from the Roman period in the parish. The first is a find of Roman pottery which is recorded in the Sites and Monuments Record as follows: "A few shards of Roman pottery, apparently found in a pipe trench dug for Bristol Waterworks Company in 1953". The location of the find is on the northern edge of Blagdon Lake, almost due south of Yeo House (see Figure 18), and the find appears to have been authenticated by Professor Rahtz. No further details are available.

The second example is more recent and more substantial, since it is now believed that there are the remains of a Roman road running through the south-east of the parish. This road was apparently first identified by John Knight of Bristol University, and has been inspected and verified by Vince Russet of North

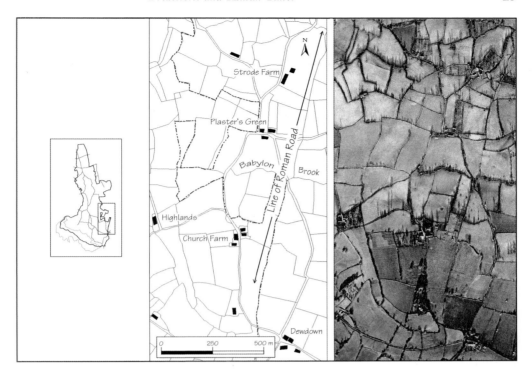

Figure 13: The Roman Road

Somerset Council and Marc Corney of Bristol University.[2] The line of the Roman road is shown in Figure 13, and appears as a straight run of hedges. It is first picked out just south-east of the church and then runs north-north-east, crossing Babylon Brook very close to where Pit Lane crosses the stream, and then up over Gravel Hill past Strode Farm. The same line reappears further north (outside the area covered by Figure 13), as a lane near Wapsell and then the main lane in Regil.

Those who have inspected this road have confirmed its Roman origins in three ways. First, its form is typical, with dead-straight sections, linked by slight kinks after which the orientation of the road may change slightly. Contrary to popular belief Roman roads do not run straight throughout their length, but tend to show slight realignments between short, straight sections. Second, where the road crosses Babylon Brook the stream has exposed the stones that made up the underpinning of the road, and it may have been that there was a bridge or ford at this point. Third, just to the north of this point, where the road climbs the hill, the hedge is markedly above the level of the field, atop a kind of bank, which is a characteristic of a situation where the hedge has been planted on an old roadway. A further circumstantial point is that the Roman road coincides with the parish boundary for about 500m (see Figure 13), as it has been argued "A genuine ancient long-distance road is nearly always a parish boundary at least in places". Those who have investigated the road say that its construction shows it to be a major road, a "Roman motorway," rather than just a local farm track. Its source and destination are unclear, but the lead mines in Mendips, and the ochre mines in Winford are possibilities.

POSSIBLE SITES: AERIAL PHOTOGRAPHY

Aerial photographs have played an important role in archaeology for nearly a century. Structures that are completely hidden below ground may show up as crop or soil marks under certain conditions, and these marks are best seen from the air. Usually differences in soil moisture, due to underground features such as the foundations of walls or disturbed earth, result in the differential growth of crops or differences in soil colour which can been seen on the photograph. Sometimes earthworks are more easily identified from the air, for example where very low banks stand out when the sunlight strikes at a particular angle.

Unfortunately soil and crop marks are often transitory, so that photographs of the same area taken at different times may show quite different results. The absence of marks therefore cannot be taken as proof that there are no hidden structures. Similarly, low banks may only be visible with the sun in a particular position. When marks are found in aerial photos excavations are necessary to prove the exact nature of the site, but experienced air-photo interpreters can make reasoned judgements of the importance of particular types of pattern. The English Heritage National Monuments Record (NMR) Centre at Swindon houses an extensive and readily accessible collection of air photographs for the country, including extensive coverage for the local area in 1946, 1960 and 1971, and there are other sources of more recent material.

When marks on aerial photography are considered of possible archaeological significance they are entered on the Sites and Monuments Record. In Nempnett Thrubwell there are five such

Figure 14: Possible Romano-British field boundaries

examples. The first of these is south of Bicknell Farm, located at ST517624, and described as "cropmarks noted from aerial photographs showing part of a field system". These cropmarks appear to be part of the Romano-British field system noted by Fowler, which is centred in Butcombe and Wrington parishes but extends eastwards into Nempnett Thrubwell in a fragmented state. Although Peter Fowler has never published a map of these fields in Nempnett he has recorded the eastern extent as being at ST525625 and the centre at ST518627 with fields for "about half a mile [700m] around this point".[3]

Figure 18 is an attempt to map the Romano-British fields in this area, based on the aerial photography shown. The top panel shows the air photograph for 4 December 1946 and is the same material as that used by Fowler in his work in Butcombe[4] (although Fowler used additional photography and ground survey as well); the bottom panel shows the 1946 field boundaries as thin lines and my suggestions for the location of old field boundaries as heavy lines.

In the aerial photograph the old field boundaries show as lines that are roughly straight (the dead-straight lines are modern drains), with a characteristic pattern of a light side to the south and darker to the north. It is likely these are very shallow banks that show up well because of the very low sun angle. Some of these are still visible today as banks or terraces, which can be seen from the footpath which runs across the centre of the area shown in Figure 14. Although there are doubtless many errors in my interpretation, Figure 14 gives some idea of the type of archaeological information that may be available from aerial photography, and how this may help to guide fieldwork.

There are four other sites on the SMR which have been derived from aerial photography, namely:

1. an oval enclosure visible as an earthwork in the north-east corner of the field, lying roughly east-west, at ST521610 (south-west of Nempnett Farm);

2. a semi-circular vegetation mark, at ST523597 (south-west of Rugmoor Farm);

3. possible earthworks, cultivation furrows, trackways and quarries or building platforms, at ST528599 (south of East House); and

4. a circular soilmark visible in the field to the south of Belvedere Manor, on the western [sic] side of the road (ST533602).

There are no further details available on any of these sites; their approximate locations are shown on Figure 18.

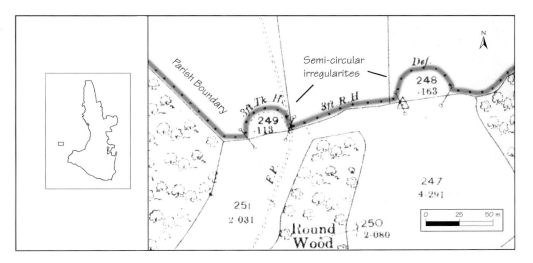

Figure 15: Irregularities in the Butcombe-Wrington Parish Boundary

IRREGULARITIES IN THE PARISH BOUNDARY

Parish boundaries are in many cases extremely old, and their boundaries tend to be very resistant to being changed. Oliver Rackham in his book *The History of the English Countryside* gives a marvellous example of irregularities in a parish boundary being the ghosts of long-forgotten landscape features. Figure 15 shows a section of the parish boundary between Butcombe and Wrington (located about 1km south-west of the Mill Inn, Butcombe) where there are two curious semi-circular irregularities. It turns out that the two deviations each represent half of a prehistoric ring-earthwork which was previously undetected; presumably over the years ploughing had removed all surface traces of archaeology, but the boundary refused to be moved, and a modern-day investigation rediscovered the ancient earthworks.[5]

There are two examples in the Nempnett Thrubwell parish boundary that are strikingly similar, where the boundary follows a particularly unusual course. The first is in the north-east corner of the parish near Kingdown – see Figure 16. The boundary between Nempnett and Winford here runs almost due north-south, but where the boundary crosses the lane there is a pronounced kink, where suddenly the boundary follows a semi-circular or "three-sides-of-a-square" diversion, as if it is "avoiding" something, creating a small "bite" out of the parish about 15m square. This

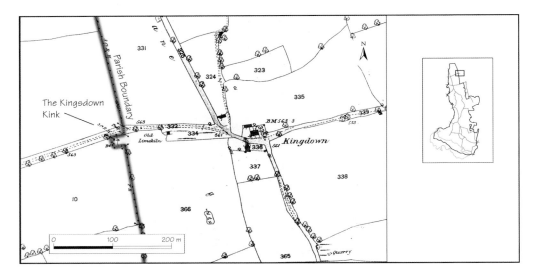

Figure 16: Parish Boundary: "Kingsdown Kink"

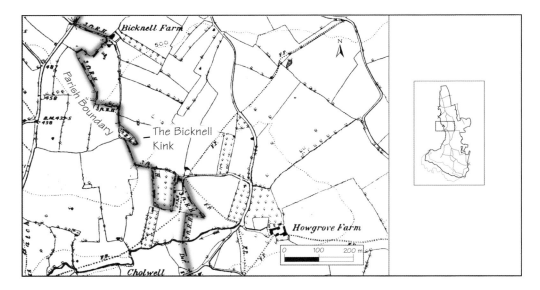

Figure 17: Parish Boundary: "Bicknell Kink"

looks quite similar to the example noted by Rackham. Could there have been an old barrow or earthwork here?

The second example is in the north-west of the parish, about 300m south of Bicknell Farm, where the parish boundary with Butcombe makes a peculiar kink – see Figure 17. Most changes

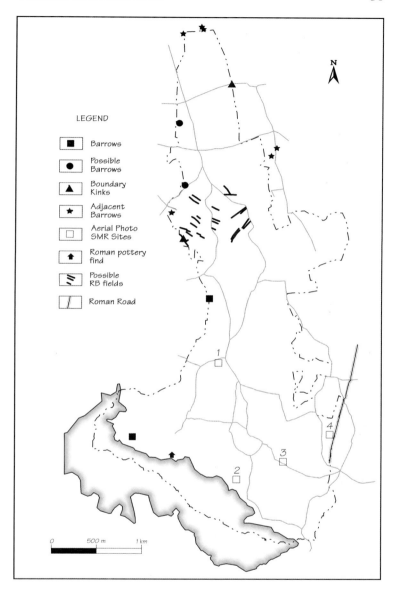

LEGEND

■ Barrows

● Possible Barrows

▲ Boundary Kinks

★ Adjacent Barrows

□ Aerial Photo SMR Sites

♠ Roman pottery find

〰 Possible RB fields

▨ Roman Road

0   500 m   1 km

Figure 18: Summary of prehistoric and Roman sites

of direction in the parish boundary are abrupt and follow field boundaries whereas this kink has rounded edges and protrudes into the middle of a field in which there is no apparent physical feature apart from a very slight bank. Again it is as if the boundary is tracing round something that is no longer there, or at least is no longer visible. This finger-like protrusion measures about 50m by 20m. Is it possible this is the site of an undiscovered long barrow?

CONCLUSION

A summary of the sites discussed in this chapter is shown in Figure 18. The earliest currently known evidence of human activity in Nempnett Thrubwell is the burial monument at Fairy's Toot, built some 5000 years ago, probably by a small group of Neolithic farmers living on the warm south-facing slopes of the parish. In the Bronze Age a number of barrows were built in and immediately adjacent to the parish, suggesting continued settlement in that period. Remnants of what are probably late Iron Age and Romano-British field systems are to be found across the north of the parish, and it quite possible that these used to be present elsewhere but that their traces have been removed by ploughing. It seems likely that a fairly major Roman road passed through the south-east corner of the parish and there has been one recorded find of Roman pottery.

As well as these definite traces of prehistoric and Roman activity, there are other examples such as soil- and crop-marks, and irregularities in parish boundary which are suggestive of prehistoric activity but whose importance remains to be assessed. Similarly in Chapter 5 there are several cases of field-names that may be of archaeological significance. Overall, it seems highly likely, given this knowledge and what is known from adjacent parishes, that Nempnett Thrubwell has been settled pretty well continuously for 5,000 years or more. But the fact that there has been so little archaeological activity in the parish means that at present we know only a tiny fraction of the story of these earliest times.

3 Fairy's Toot

INTRODUCTION

This chapter discusses in more detail the story of Fairy's Toot, a Neolithic long barrow built in the parish some 5,000 years ago, the earliest known trace of human settlement in Nempnett. When first built, and for many centuries after, the Toot was a substantial feature, about 50m long by 25m wide and 5m high. Unfortunately it was almost totally destroyed in the early 19th century and today there is little remaining to see. However, the site is still considered of sufficient importance to be a scheduled monument protected under Section I of the Ancient Monuments and Archaeological Areas Act of 1979.

Fairy's Toot takes its common name, like many ancient tombs, from a long held belief that it was the focus of supernatural activities, the word *toot* being an old name for hill, so that the name means "the hill of the fairies." In his book *The History and Antiquities of the County of Somersetshire*, published in 1791, John Collinson says that

> since time immemorial the field has been called Fairy Field: the common people say that strange noises have been heard under the hill, and visions portentous to children have been seen waving in the thickets which crown its summit.

In her book *The Archaeology of Somerset*, published in 1931, Dina Dobson describes a visit to the site thus: "the young man of the village who was first asked as to its whereabouts knew

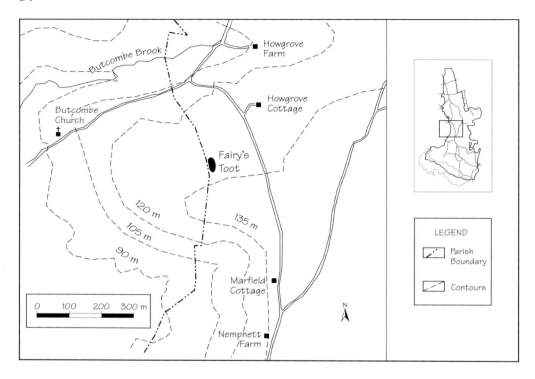

Figure 19: Fairy's Toot location map

nothing of its existence, but an elderly labourer pointed the way, and said that the fairies still lived in its underground chambers".[1] And these legends continue, although they are modified to fit the times. In 2001 an elderly resident told me that when he was at school there were tales of how fairies on horseback could be seen and heard crossing the lane by the Toot. And the children of nearby residents still treat a visit to the Toot as a somewhat scary experience, especially if they are "lucky" enough to be allowed to camp there overnight.

The Toot was largely demolished between 1787 and 1835, but two Victorian parsons, Thomas Bere of Butcombe and John Skinner of Camerton, explored and recorded the site before its destruction. The writings of Bere and Skinner, combined with more recent archaeological work on similar tombs, mean we now know with reasonable certainty when it was built and what it looked like in its original form. Also a great deal of archaelogical work has tried to answer the questions as to why it was built in the first place and how it might have been used.

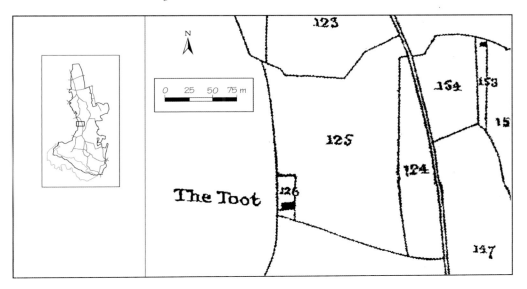

Figure 20: Extract from the 1841 Tithe Map showing Fairy's Toot

LOCATION

Fairy's Toot is situated about 150m west of the lane that runs from Nempnett Farm northwards towards Howgrove Farm and Butcombe, at OS grid reference ST521618 – see Figure 19. It lies at about 130m above sea level, just off the crest of a hill (previously known as Hooks or Rooks Hill) on a gentle north-facing slope with extensive views to the west and north, while to the east is the higher plateau land of Broadfield Down.

The Toot lies immediately adjacent to the parish boundary between Nempnett Thrubwell and Butcombe, and this has been the cause of some confusion. In John Rutter's *Delineations of Somersetshire* it is referred to as Butcombe Barrow and an authoritative work on Somerset barrows by Leslie Grinsell also locates it in Butcombe parish. The fact that the parish boundary passes so close to the Toot is unlikely to be a coincidence, as discussed in Chapter 2.

The first detailed parish map on which the Toot appeared was the 1841 Tithe Map - see Figure 20. On the map solid lines denote field boundaries, hedges, or fences, and buildings are shaded, so that the site of the Toot appears to have been fenced off and a farm building constructed, which appears to be the barn part of which is still standing today. The field was at that

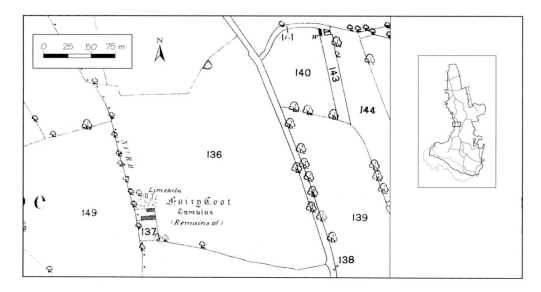

Figure 21: Extract from the 1884 Ordnance Survey first edition showing Fairy's Toot

time owned by Maria Moulton and farmed by Benjamin Warford, as were the fields to the east and south. As the Tithe Map covers only Nempnett parish, the area to the west of the Toot is blank being in Butcombe parish.

The first edition of the Ordnance Survey map, surveyed in 1884 and published in 1885, shows the area in more detail – see Figure 21. The area of the Toot is fenced off in some way, and this "field" is labelled 137. In the centre of the field is a large building measuring about 13m by 3m. The OS map also shows a much smaller building in the north-east corner of the "Toot field", about 7m by 3m in size. Just to the north is a limekiln that appears to be a very small rectangular structure, and around this are symbols for a rough area of stone.

The field labelled 136 in Figure 21 has since been amalgamated with the field to the south, so that today the Toot lies near the mid-point of the western edge of a fourteen-acre field. The boundary that separated the small field around the Toot has gone and sheep graze the site, thus keeping down shrubs. From a distance the site looks like a small copse – Plate 9 shows the view from the east.

A visit to the site today gives a sense of the scale of the original monument and its fine setting. There is little to see on the surface but a rectangular area covered with stone rubble, mostly about

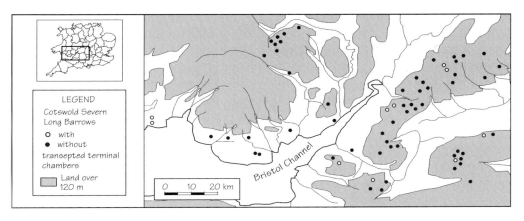

Figure 22: Distribution map of Cotswold-Severn tombs (after Daniel 1950, p65)

the size of household bricks, although there are some larger slabs, like paving stones, some of the order of 1m square by 0.1m thick. On the site are about six established beech and ash trees and at the northern end there are two quite substantial mounds of the rubble about 1 or 2m high. By the north-east mound there is some dry stone walling, which is most likely a remnant of the limekiln. A stone barn was constructed in the centre of the site around 1830, orientated east-west, and two walls of this are still standing. The site is on private land but can be seen from the lane.

FAIRY'S TOOT: A COTSWOLD-SEVERN LONG BARROW

Archaeologists have been able to classify Fairy's Toot using the memoirs of Thomas Bere and John Skinner, and are now certain it was a type of long barrow, that is to say a burial chamber, dating from the Early or Middle Neolithic period, sometime between 4000BC and 3200 BC. Fairy's Toot belongs to a type of long barrow known as Cotswold-Severn tombs, which are found in South Wales, Hereford, Gloucestershire, Somerset, Wiltshire, Oxford, and Berkshire; one estimate of their geographical distribution is shown in Figure 22, although there is still much debate over the classification of various sites. A more detailed map for part of the northern Somerset region is shown in Figure 23. [2]

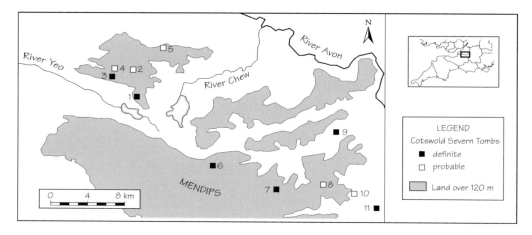

Figure 23: Cotswold-Severn tombs in north Somerset: 1: Fairys' Toot, 2: Felton Hill, 3: Red Hill, 4: The Waterstone, 5: Soldier's Grave, 6: Chew Down, 7: Charmborough Hill, 8: Buckland Down, 9 Stoney Littleton, 10: Murtry Hill, 11: Fromefield (after Corcoran 1969, p25)

The distinctive feature of the Cotswold-Severn long barrows is that they have internal chambers in which the remains of the dead were buried – like a set of small catacombs. These chambers were constructed from a combination of large, flat slabs of stone, known as megaliths or orthostats, and smaller irregular brick-sized stones. Further sub-divisions of the Cotswold-Severn group are made on the basis of the shape and form of these internal chambers. Fairy's Toot is now believed to have belonged to a sub-group called "with transepted terminal chambers" (although Thurnam uses the more accessible term "chambers opening into a central gallery"). This is the most elaborate of the sub-groups, and relatively rare.

An attempt to show what a newly finished "typical" Cotswold-Severn tomb with transepted terminal chambers would have looked like is given in Figure 24. From the outside the overall form of the cairn was a long oval mound or trapezoid, with one end of the long axis having an entrance or forecourt to the internal chambers. The cairn was usually broader and higher at the entrance end (rather than being symmetrical). Sizes varied, with lengths varying from 12m to 90m, the most common length being around 50m, with the width typically a third of the length, although more circular cairns also exist. There was usually an extremely well made dry stone wall revetment about 1m in height surrounding the cairn.

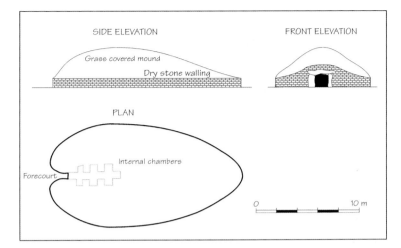

Figure 24: "Typical" Cotswold-Severn tomb with transepted terminal chambers

The entrance was contained within a sweeping forecourt defined by projecting "horns" from the main mound. The doorway itself varied in height from 0.8 to 1.2m, was often square, and was usually extremely imposing and well-built, using stones which were "for the most part, of larger and more massive proportions than any of the others used in the composition of the chambers". The surrounding stone walling increased in height at the doorway to combine with these megaliths to form an imposing entrance forecourt around the door.

The internal chambers were constructed from a combination of megaliths and smaller stones, a technique known as "alternate orthostat and drystone walling." The megaliths were typically square in shape, about 1m wide and high, but quite thin, typically 0.1m or less; they were set in threes, as at Stonehenge, with two vertical and one across the top, so as to form a passageway about 1m square. Gaps between the megaliths were then filled up with smaller stones, similar to those used in the surrounding dry stone walling. In cairns with "terminal transepted chambers" there was a central passage set on the long axis of the cairn with side chambers that opened from the central passage arranged in pairs "in the manner of transepts in some Christian churches." The side chambers, sometimes called cists, are usually *c.* 1m in depth, width, and height and are formed by sets of the large stones.

The consensus among experts seems to be that, while the tombs were still being used for burials, the entrance to the chambers would have been blocked in some way, probably by a large stone or stones. It is assumed that these blocks served to keep out unwanted visitors, human or animal, and would have been removed and replaced as the need for access demanded. Fairy's Toot appears to have used a particularly unusual form of blocking, known as a porthole. A porthole entrance has been defined as an artificially-constructed hole large enough to allow the tomb to be entered in a creeping posture, and which occurs at the entrance to the tomb to restrict and demarcate the entrance to the burial chamber. Occurrences of portholes are extremely rare.

When the cairn ceased to be used for burial most experts believe that it was then more carefully and permanently sealed, often with a secondary blocking stone at the entrance to the chamber and further blocking-up of the wider forecourt, although there are some who argue that this later blocking is due only to natural weathering and collapse. Examples of internal blocking, that is the filling of the internal chambers with material, are also known.

STONEY LITTELTON: A SURVIVING COTSWOLD-SEVERN TOMB

One of the best-preserved examples of a Cotswold-Severn barrow with terminal transepted chambers is to be found at Stoney Littleton, just south-west of Wellow, at OS grid reference ST735572, about 10km to the south-east of Fairy's Toot. Not only is Stoney Littleton worth a visit in its own right, but it also the closest we have today of a recreation of what Fairy's Toot might have been like in its original state. Those who knew both barrows in the 19th century commented on their similarity: John Skinner says that the Fairy's Toot sepulchre "was exactly similar to that at Stoney Littleton, only on a larger scale",[3] and the Rev Samuel Seyer says Stoney Littleton is "so nearly resembling Fairy's Toot in every particular, that the same description would be sufficient for both".[4]

John Skinner and the respected archaeologist Sir Richard Colt Hoare investigated Stoney Littleton in 1816. At this time the barrow was apparently in a reasonable state of repair, although it had been opened in the mid-18th century when the local farmer "carried away many cartloads of stones for the roads". In 1858 Stoney Littleton was completely restored, under the auspices of the Lord of the Hundred Mr. T R Joliffe, so that "the design

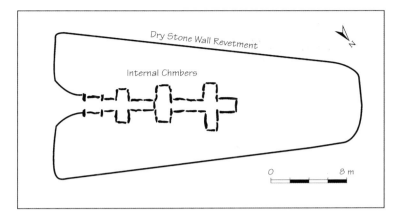

Figure 25: Stoney Littleton plan (after Grinsell 1982)

of the original structure [was].. preserved, as far as possible, with scrupulous exactness." Stoney Littleton is now under the guardianship of English Heritage and has recently been repaired to ensure it is structurally sound; it is now open to the public with the central passageway and chambers fully accessible. Some visitors have suggested that the site be renamed "Muddy Littleton", so be warned.

A view of the Stoney Littleton barrow showing the entrance is shown in Plate 10, a plan of the mound and the internal chambers in Figure 25, and a photograph taken inside the barrow of one of the cists in Plate 11. The structure as a whole is about 30m long, 15m wide at its broadest and 2-3m high, which puts it at the smaller end of the known range of sizes. A dry stone wall about 1m in height built of small brick-sized stones retains it, a typical revetment. The central passageway measures about 15m in length, and is typically 1m in height. There are three pairs of chambers leading off the central way, each of which is about 1m in depth, width, and height. When the interior of the tomb was opened in 1816 there were found many human remains, including "four jaw-bones, the teeth perfect... the upper part of two crania, which appeared to us remarkably flat in the forehead... several leg, thigh and arm bones... and confused piles of bones".

The passage and chambers are built of a mixture of large slabs and smaller stone, with the largest slabs to be found at the entrance where the lintel is about 2.1m in length. The left-hand upright of the trilithon that forms the entrance has a fine impression of an ammonite about 0.3m in diameter suggesting that special care was taken in choosing and setting the doorway stones. Geological analysis of the stones used has shown them to be of two sorts: the smaller stones are Forest Marble limestone, the nearest source of which is about 1km from the barrow, and the larger stones, or megaliths, are Blue Lias slabs, the nearest outcrop of which is at Newton St. Loe about 8km away.

THEORIES OF THE USES OF COTSWOLD-SEVERN TOMBS

Although it is possible to build up a fairly accurate picture of the original form of a Cotswold-Severn tomb, the debates about why they were built and how they were used have continued for a century and a half. At first this debate was largely based upon the descriptions of the form and typology of the tombs, but more recently significant archaeological evidence has been provided from a number of extensive modern excavations at a few well-preserved sites. Of particular note are the excavations by Alan Saville at Hazelton North in Gloucestershire, an almost undisturbed Cotswold-Severn barrow.

There is no doubt that the primary function concerned the dead. When these tombs have been excavated human remains have been found, as noted at Stoney Littleton. At Hazleton North, one of the few tombs where accurate figures are available, remains of 21 adults and 12-19 pre-adults were discovered, and these figures are comparable with other recent excavations. Although older accounts are much less precise, they do suggest that the numbers of individuals found is measured in dozens, rather than hundreds, and Saville concludes "there are no indications that Cotswold-Severn tombs ever contained more than 50 individuals." The bones are usually found "disarticulated and thoroughly mixed," rather than as neatly laid out complete skeletons. The remains are generally unburnt and other finds such as pottery and artefacts are scarce.

There are two theories about the period of time over which these tombs were used. Until recently the consensus was that the barrows were in use for very long periods, perhaps as much as a 1,000 years. This reflected the belief that they were the final resting place of only certain privileged members of the community. Saville has suggested a much shorter period of use, on the basis of his very detailed work at Hazleton North; he says:

"the burial evidence is interpreted as being consistent with the interment of individuals, irrespective of age or sex, within the chambered areas at or soon after the time of their death…. There is no need to envisage the Hazleton burials as anything other than the collective dead of a small scale local community".[5]

He suggests that tombs may have been in use for as little as 100 years or less, with the communities as small as 8-24 people.

A number of studies have been undertaken to estimate the amount of effort necessary to build a Cotswold-Severn tomb. The figures are generally in the region of 8,000-14,000 work hours. These figures are high in the sense that they underline the degree of commitment and organisation needed to complete a tomb, but 6 individuals working 20 hours each a week would complete the task in 3-4 months. Since the tomb would not have necessarily been completed within a single season it is quite possible to have been the result of the actions of a very small community.

There is agreement amongst archaeologists that the Cotswold-Severn tombs must also have served a ritual purpose. The burial chambers form only a very small part of the monument as a whole, typically around 7%, suggesting they were not built "just" as burying places but had a monumental or ritual function too. It has been noted that the front elevation of the "typical" cairn (as shown in Figure 24) is strikingly house-like so that the intention might have been to produce a "house of the dead", a copy in durable stone of the timber-built house of the living, with particular emphasis put on the doorway.[6]

Current theory and research also suggests that Neolithic people used the bones of the ancestors in some form of open-air ritual ceremonies. The stone built chambers would have been an excellent way of preserving these bones, and protecting them from unwanted predators, and would have been a natural focus for such activities.[7] Excavations of the entrance area in other Cotswold-Severn tombs have uncovered remains of animals, especially pigs and cattle, suggesting that the forecourt was used for "ritual slaughter and feasting".[8]

The tombs may also have served as territorial markers, as emblems of the social groups that constructed them, which bound the group together and signalled to other groups their presence and validated their use of the land.[9] In other words they were a statement that this piece of land was "taken" or "owned" by a group who could call on the power of their ancestors against unwanted intruders.

Although it will probably never be possible to determine the importance and detail of ritual uses, it seems agreed that some such use would have accompanied these monuments, and these symbolic uses probably explain why early groups were prepared to spend so much time and care on their construction.

THE DESTRUCTION OF FAIRY'S TOOT

The destruction of Fairy's Toot in the late-18th and early-19th centuries is a sorry tale, but not an unusual one. A combination of the need for stone for parish roads and the making of lime, the ready availability of suitable stone in the Toot, and a general lack of interest in antiquities led to the Toot being razed to the ground. Unfortunately, there are many similar stories from the same period. Writing in the 1820s John Skinner says that of five other nearby barrows of similar type to Fairy's Toot four have been "almost wholly removed" or "nearly obliterated from the face of the earth".[10]

The story of the Toot's demise begins in 1789. Mr. Gray, a local farmer and waywarden, employed some workmen to obtain stones from the tumulus in order to repair the parish roads. The "plundering" or "recycling" of barrow stone for this reason was common in the period 1790 to 1830, and the same thing is known to have happened at nearby barrows at Buckland Dinham, Camerton, Priddy and Stoney Littleton.[11] A few years later a limekiln was built adjacent to Fairy's Toot to burn the (remaining) stones, with the lime which resulted being used to manufacture mortar and plaster for building or to improve the soil. This use of the stone from barrows was also common, and is known to have happened at Priddy and Priston.

By 1835 the tumulus had been almost totally destroyed. In *The History and Antiquities of Somersetshire*, published in 1836-9, W Phelps writes "the whole tumulus is now (1835) nearly destroyed; a lime-kiln having been built on the spot, and the stones burnt into lime".[12] On 17 July 1856 the Reverend Scarth visited the site and "found the whole an entire ruin, no other trace of the tumulus left than a few heaps of small stones near the lime-kiln, which seems to have been disused for some time".[13]

Whereas Sir Richard Colt Hoare made very accurate drawings and plans of Stoney Littleton when it was excavated in the early 19th century, no such detailed drawings survive for Fairy's Toot. Indeed the very opposite is true, as the accounts of the discovery and subsequent investigation of Fairy's Toot are "vague and often contradictory". However, a careful re-examination of the accounts of Thomas Bere and John Skinner in the light of current day knowledge of Cotswold-Severn tombs in general, and of Stoney Littleton in particular, does allow us to reconstruct with some accuracy what Fairy's Toot was like when it was first built.

THOMAS BERE'S ACCOUNTS OF FAIRY'S TOOT

Thomas Bere was the first to write about Fairy's Toot, but relatively little is known about him as a man. He was rector of Butcombe from 1781 to 1814, one of His Majesty's Justices of the Peace for the County of Somerset, and was married. He was clearly an educated man, as he refers widely to the classics, and writes in both Latin and Greek. Bere is probably most widely known for his clash with Hannah More over her charity schools in the neighbourhood of Mendip, which he accused of "holding conventicles, using extemporare prayer, hearing oral confessions, and introducing Methodism." [14] Bere died on 28 October 1814 and is buried in Bathampton. His obituary in *The Western Flying Post* says "his orthodox principles as a member of the established church, and his upright conduct as a magistrate, added to a cheerful and affectionate disposition, will long endear his memory to a large circle of friends and acquaintance."

Bere's first communication about Fairy's Toot was a short letter in *The Bath Chronicle* of 1789. He describes the size of the barrow and the early findings that had come to light when Mr. Gray began to obtain stones from the tumulus. In Bere's own words he published this letter

> "in [the] hope of attracting the attention of some gentleman who, from knowledge in ancient history, might have been able to give the public information, or probable conjecture at least, relative to this new species of sepulchral monument. To invite investigation, I subjoined my address; and happy should I have been in giving every

information or assistance my locality afforded me to such a one ."

But no-one took up Bere's well intentioned offer, and, since he recognised the extraordinary nature of the barrow, he took it upon to himself to publish a more detailed record of the barrow and the excavations "rather than suffer so curious a discovery to pass back into the regions of oblivion, without that respect which, I am persuaded, its singular construction demands".

To give more details of his find Bere published two longer letters in *The Gentleman's Magazine* in 1789 and 1792. The first gives a detailed account of the barrow and the excavations there, and includes the drawing that is reproduced as Figure 26. This diagram has been criticised by some as a "very inadequate and confusing illustration",[15] but it is better than nothing and something that deserves consideration.

Bere does not appear to have been a draughtsman or archaeologist, and part of the problem is that the drawing is both a general view of the barrow and an attempt to record what was found when it was excavated. The use of letters in the drawing, which are referred to in the text, makes it somewhat confusing, and the perspective also looks wrong. It would certainly have been better to draw a series of sketches illustrating different aspects of the barrow. However, careful examination of the drawing, in conjunction with Bere's written account and what is now known about Cotswold-Severn tombs, shows that it contains much valuable information.

The view is taken from the east, showing the barrow covered with turf, bushes, and trees. The left hand side is south, and this is the entrance or forecourt end. The profile of the barrow is asymmetric, with the highest point nearer the southern, entrance end, as is the case in other similar tombs (see the side elevation in Figure 24). Bere measures the barrow as "from North to South 150 feet [46m], from East to West 75 feet [23m]."

Mr. Gray's workmen had made two excavations into the Toot, one at the southern extremity, the other along the eastern side, both of which are shown in "cut-away" style on the drawing. For clarity Figures 27 and 28 show in enlarged form these parts of the diagram. Bere describes the "southern excavation" as follows: "Desirous of obtaining stone for the adjacent roads, the proprietor ordered his workmen to see what the Toote was made of. They accordingly commenced their labours at the Southern

Figure 26: Thomas Bere's 1789 drawing of Fairy's Toot

extremity, and soon came to the stone D, which then was at A, with a considerable West inclination." This "enormous flat stone" was "6ft. [1.8m] long (high), 5ft. [1.5m] broad, and 16ins [0.14m] thick."

Bere suggests that this stone "no doubt served for a door to the sepulchre, which, prior (and in some instances subsequent) to Christianity, was the common mode of securing the entrance of their repositories. Such was that which was placed at the mouth of the cave wherein our blessed Saviour was interred." In a way he was right, as the modern interpretation of a Cotswold Severn tomb would be that the area from A to B was the forecourt and that the stone D was part of a final blocking-up or sealing of the forecourt which would have taken place after the tomb had been used for the last time.

Bere continues, the "stone D being passed, an admirable unmortar'd wall appeared on the left-hand, and no doubt a similar one after the dotted line on the right once existed". The wall he found is shown at H in Figures 26 and 27, to the right of which is the dotted line running up to the letter I. "This wall was built

Figure 27: Detail of the southern excavation from Thomas Bere's 1789 drawing of Fairy's Toot

of thin irregular bate freestone, less in length and breadth, but in general thicker, than common Dutch chimney tile. Its height was somewhat more than four feet [1.2m]; its thickness about fourteen inches [0.12m]." What Bere appears to be describing here is a typical Cotswold Severn forecourt, about 4m long, with the wall increasing in height towards the entrance, as at Stoney Littleton (see Plate 10 and Figure 24).

What Bere came to next appears to be a porthole entrance to the inside of the tomb: "Thirteen feet [4m] directly North from A (where the stone D stood) the perforated stone B appears, inclining to the North about thirty degrees, and shutting up the avenue between the unmortar'd walls." The size of stone B is not given, but assuming it was of comparable size to stone D and that the diagram is roughly drawn to scale, the hole within it is likely to have been at least 0.8m wide and 0.5m high.

Bere managed to work his way round the porthole stone and then "at I a cell presented itself, two feet three inches [0.23m] broad, four feet [1.2m] high and nine feet [2.7m] from South to North. Here were found a perfect human skull, the teeth entire, all sound, and of the most delicate white: it lay against the inside of the stone B, the body having been deposited North and South. Several other pieces of skulls, human spinal joints, arm bones etc. were found herein; and particularly the thigh bone of a very large quadruped, which, by comparing with the same bone of an ox, I conjecture to have belonged to an animal of that species....

Figure 28: Detail of the eastern excavation from Thomas Bere's 1789 drawing of Fairy's Toot

In this cell was also found the tooth of some large beast; but no one that has seen it can guess of what genus." From the description, this "cell" or "first sepulchre" appears to be part of a central avenue and the body laid there was probably the last to be interred before the final sealing up of the tomb.

Bere then ran into problems: "At the termination of the first sepulchre, the horizontal stones in the top of the avenue had fallen down. With some difficulty, and no little danger, I obtruded far enough to see, by the light of a candle, two other similar catacombs, one on the right, the other on the left side of the avenue, containing several human skulls, and other bones; but which, from the imminent hazard of being buried in the ruins of the surrounding masses, have not yet been entered." It seems that what Bere saw here was the first pair of chambers leading off the central avenue, but he could see no further along the passageway.

The work at the eastern side of the barrow produced rather less in the way of finds but was important in that it established the extent of the internal structure of the barrow (see Figure 28). Bere describes the finds as follows: "The lateral section at G has afforded as yet nothing more than a view of the unmortar'd wall, seen in the Southern extremity at H, and here at F". It seems likely that the stone wall at F is like the revetment type found at Stoney Littleton that had over the centuries become covered with soil through the natural processes of erosion.

Then Bere found the "continuation of the central avenue seen at B, and here from C to C." He described its thus: "This avenue

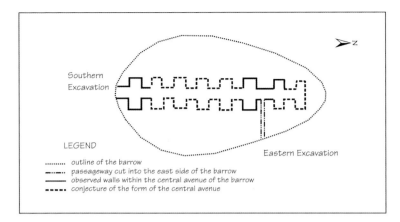

Figure 29: Thomas Bere's plan or iconography of Fairy's Toot, 1792

is constructed of very large rock fragments, consisting of three stones, two perpendicular and one horizontal, as may be seen in the representation E (see Figure 26 where the diagrammatic representation "E" appears in the lower left). Three cells are here discernible, two of which are on the West side, and one on the East; these also have human bones..." An annoying omission of the account is that there is no indication of how far the eastern excavation is from the southern end of the barrow, so that the length of the central avenue cannot be gauged with any accuracy.

Bere has some more general comments on the barrow. He notes that "the tumulus is formed of small whitish stone, of which the neighbourhood affords plenty, and that the exterior appears to have been turfed, there yet remains a stratum, five or six inches [0.05m] deep, of grassed earth on the stones." Unfortunately Bere does not comment on the nature of the very large rock fragments other than noting that the huge entrance stone D was "of the same specific gravity, colour and stratum" as the very large rocks exposed in the eastern transect used for the construction of the internal chambers.

Bere's second letter to *The Gentleman's Magazine* is mainly concerned with speculations about the origins of the barrow, but it also includes a plan, or iconography as Bere calls it, of the interior of the barrow, which is shown in Figure 29. Unfortunately, this diagram probably helped to confuse matters rather than clarify them. The plan shows the parts of the barrow Bere explored, and speculates about the remainder of its interior, but there is no scale and the plan is not consistent with the written account of

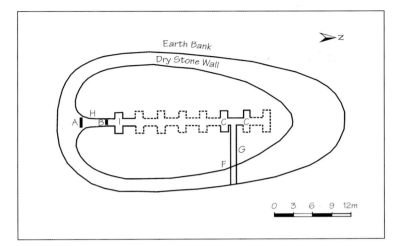

Figure 30: Arthur Bulleid's 1941 redrawing of Thomas Bere's plan

1789. Why Bere chose to show there being 8 pairs of internal chambers is also not clear.

In 1941 Arthur Bulleid published a redrawn plan to be consistent with Bere's written account, as shown in Figure 30. This shows more clearly the nature of the forecourt, running from A (where the large stone D was found) to B (the porthole stone) and bounded by the dry stone wall H. The area between the dry stone wall and the earth bank is likely to have been filled by the natural processes of erosion. The letter I marks where the final skeleton was laid against the porthole stone. The eastern excavation is at G, which passed the revetment wall at F and uncovered further chambers at C. The drawing also has 8 pairs of chambers, but there must be an element of doubt about this aspect of the drawing, as Bere did not record exactly where the eastern work took place. In most Cotswold-Severn tombs the internal chambers do not run right through the barrow; for example, at Stoney Littleton the central passageway is only just over half the length of the barrow (as shown in Figure 25).

Bere had hopes of carrying out further work at the barrow: "The proprietor means now to proceed [by].. propping up the avenue with wooden posts, in the same manner in which our miners do their adits, to the lapis caluminatis veins. This mode will give the visitor an opportunity of seeing the different cells with safety and convenience." However, in his 1792 letter he says "I am sorry now to inform you, that very little progress has been made; nor is there at present much probability of the interior recesses being speedily explored" and there are no further communications from Bere about the matter.

We should be deeply indebted to Thomas Bere for his letters and the notes and drawings he made regarding Fairy's Toot. Leslie Grinsell, perhaps the most respected writer on Somerset barrows, notes how Bere "carefully watched and archaeologically recorded" the barrow,[16] an unusual occurrence at this time. Arthur Bulleid, another local expert, says "Bere did his utmost to draw the attention of people to its importance and value, but his letters failed to attract help or any advice. In his day antiquaries were scarce and the preservation of such relics did not interest the general public".[17]

JOHN SKINNER'S ACCOUNTS OF FAIRY'S TOOT

The second visitor to Fairy's Toot was the rather better known historical figure, Reverend John Skinner. Born in 1772, he was rector of Camerton from 1800 to 1839 and was also an active antiquarian and diarist. The assessment of his contribution to archaeology is mixed. He left over 100 volumes of papers, including 9,000 sketches, mostly in the British Library, which often provide unique evidence of the state of barrows in the early 19th century. On the other hand "he was far too fond of the casual employment of miners from the north Somerset coalfields to open barrows, work for which almost all of them were totally unsuited. Skinner himself gave very little supervision .. [and he] had the regrettable tendency to present lady friends with beads and any other objects of female adornment which he found in barrows".[18] His troubled life ended with his suicide on 12 October 1839, and his journals recount many aspects of his life and times.

Skinner's first visit to Fairy's Toot was on 4 August 1820. It was a busy day. He started at Cheddar, but due to heavy rain could not leave until 11 am. He then went over the Mendips, sketching Cheddar and the view from the summit, visited Burrington church and lunched at Blagdon. He stopped at Butcombe church before arriving at Fairy's Toot, visited Ubley church afterwards, and then returned home to Camerton. His diary for the day contains many descriptions, sketches, and speculations on various aspects of the countryside and its churches.

Skinner describes his visit to the Toot thus:

"Then turning to the right [from Butcombe Church], as we gained the higher ground, and pursued a narrow lane, it bought us to the barrow; which like that at Stoney Littleton, was of an oval shape, but of larger dimensions, measuring about 42 yards [38m] in length, and 40 feet [12m] across; half of the super structure has been removed, leaving some of the stones which formed the cists; the other part, about 10 or 12 feet [3.0-3.7m] in height, retains some Ash trees growing on the Tumulus". [19]

Skinner uses the term "cist" for the internal chambers such as were found at tombs like Fairy's Toot and Stoney Littleton, and sometimes refers to this type of burial monument as a "cisted barrow."

The visit must have been quite a short one, given Skinner's itinerary for the day, and his main intention seems to have been to record the site. He drew four sketches (reproduced in Figure 31) which show that about half the northern end of the barrow had by then been removed. The way the large stones are shown alongside a workman allows one to judge their size, which must have been of the order of 1m square, of similar size to the megaliths used at Stoney Littleton. The sketch of the southern end shows a more elaborate wall-like structure, built of stones of a similar size, which would appear to be an entrance to the tomb, although no clear opening is shown. The views from the south-east and south-west give an indication of the scale of the barrow, and show a small building at one extremity.

He also drew a rough ground plan reproduced in Figure 32 This records that the tumulus was 42 paces in length, and appears to show that about half the tumulus had been removed, at the northern end. The plan gives an indication of the size of some of the larger stones which lay scattered about, presumably waiting to be removed. There is some very faint lettering adjacent to these stones which appears to read something like "Lysham" or "Dyham". At the southern end there is a faint wavy line running across the barrow, perhaps suggesting this end had been altered too, but just how is not clear. Although the plan and sketches give much information about the state of the barrow in 1820 there are some inconsistencies. In his diary, Skinner says the barrow was 40ft wide [12m] and 42 yards [38m] long but the plan suggests it is half as wide as it is long, so either the plan and/or these measurements must be approximate.

The South End of Fairy Toot

North End of Fairy Toot Barrow

Figure 31: John Skinner's 1820 sketches of Fairy's Toot (part 1)

Further information about the history of the barrow is also recorded in the diary. Skinner writes:

"On our way to Butcombe I fell in with a young man, a native of the place, who said he perfectly remembered when there was an opening to the burying place at Fairy Toot; that people went into it by a kind of passage, having recesses on each side, in which the skeletons of the dead remained interred; but now the passage was closed up by the falling of the stones out of the heap, and that quantities had been removed for the sake of building and clearing the ground".[20]

South West view of Fairy Toot

South East Side of the Tumulus with ash tree growing on it

Figure 31: (part 2)

It seems likely this young man had been present at Bere's excavation, and his account of the collapse of the entrance would explain why Skinner's sketch of the southern end of the barrow shows no such opening.

Skinner returned to Fairy's Toot on 21 August 1822. This was a longer visit and he was intent on excavating the interior of the tomb. Thus he records:

> "We proceeded through Butcombe to Fairy Toot, enlisting by the way some workmen, armed at all points with pickaxes and shovels for the purpose of making an opening for the examination of the interior".[21]

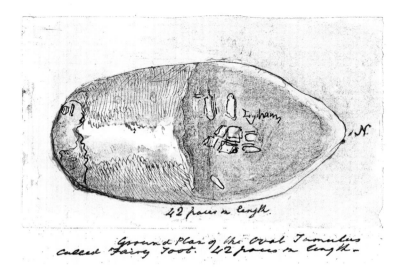

Figure 32: John Skinner's 1820 ground plan of Fairy's Toot

They started at the northern end but "as I perceived, the vaulted passage had been much injured by the throwing down of the covering stones at the northern entrance and no passage could be procured." It is notable that Skinner does not discuss the state of the barrow, which, judging by his visit in 1820, must have been at least half removed.

At the southern end he was more successful:

> "I desired the labourers to try at the opposite extremity, and after two hours exertion, found the same impediment, the stones which formed the covering, or roof of the passage having fallen down; but I saw enough to satisfy me this sepulchre was exactly similar to that at Stoney Littleton, only on a larger scale, as it probably contained six cists on a side, and one at each end, making fourteen compartments, whereas Stoney Littleton Barrow had but eight".[22]

Skinner drew two sketches while this work was going on, which are reproduced in Figure 33. In the upper drawing of the entrance to the tomb the human figures help give a sense of scale, and the largest of the stones shown here reaches almost to the workman's shoulder and so must be of the order of 1.5m high; other stones of slightly smaller size are also shown. In his diary he notes that the "stones were some of them three tons [in] weight."

Figure 33: John Skinner's 1822 sketches of Fairy's Toot

There is also a sketch of the ground plan of the barrow, as shown in Figure 34. This shows six pairs of cists, or chambers, and how the cists were made up of large stones (cf. Figure 25, which shows a similar plan for Stoney Littleton). It also appears to show a blocking stone at the leftmost (southern) end of the central passageway, where Bere reported the porthole stone, and that the leftmost pair of cists is blocked off from the central avenue.

The ground plan appears to show the outline of the barrow, marked by short hatch marks, with the internal chambers extending throughout the length of the barrow. This might be speculation or poetic licence. Assuming each cist was about 1.5m

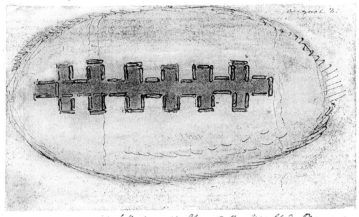

Called Fairy Toot with the cists in which the bodies were placed in

Figure 34: John Skinner's 1822 ground plan of Fairy's Toot

wide, with another 1.5m or so between each pair of cists, the length of the internal chambers would be approximately 21m, while the length of the barrow was 38m. Thus, if the drawing were to scale the chambers would only occupy half the length of the barrow, an arrangement that would be consistent with what is known of other Cotswold-Severn tombs.

Skinner again gathered important information about the barrow from a local man, which he records in his diary thus:

> "An old man, Clerk of Butcombe, perfectly well remembered when it [the Toot] was opened, and says, some of the skeletons were found in a sitting posture; their heads supported in the corner of the cists; he never heard them speak of any weapons or ornaments having been placed near the bodies, and from four or five might have been in each cist".[23]

This account seems similar to that given by Bere, in terms of there being many human remains but few other grave goods, but whether the apparently more accurate account of the skeletons being found "in a sitting posture, four or five to a cist" reflects the results of further unrecorded excavations is not known.

Skinner also procured "a portion of one of the skulls" which he noted "is of extraordinary thickness, and but little injured by time". This fragment of skull, which measures about 10cm

Figure 35: Fragment of a human skull found at Fairy's Toot

by 8cm and is shown in Figure 35, was passed to Bristol City Museum in 1839 as part of the Skinner Collection, although it was not catalogued until 1923. It is said to be a fragment of the left parietal bone, but it is not possible to tell whether it is from a male or female.[24] Who was responsible for the engraving on the skull is not known, but the label F779 is the museum "register number." Regarding the other remains, the Rev Scarth said in 1858 "it is a subject of great regret, that of the many skulls said to have been found in the Butcombe tumulus [Fairy's Toot], none should have been preserved, as far as we know".

Skinner's visits to Fairy's Toot seem fairly typical of his activities, characterised by enthusiasm and hard work, but not as methodical as modern day archaeologists would like. His talent for sketching means we have extensive pictorial records of the state of the Toot around 1820, and his diaries provide valuable information including the memories of local people. The main problem of Skinner's work is that, like Bere, he was only able to guess at the original internal structure of the Toot. His ground plan (Figure 34) is very similar to Bere's (Figure 29) and from 1820 onwards this type of ground plan seems to have been used by subsequent writers as a "true" representation of Fairy's Toot.

LATER ACCOUNTS OF FAIRY'S TOOT

After Thomas Bere and John Skinner recorded and published details of Fairy's Toot, reports of it began to appear in more general publications. In some cases additional "details" were added, although often without explanation. In this way the story of Fairy's Toot became more complex, and separating the myth

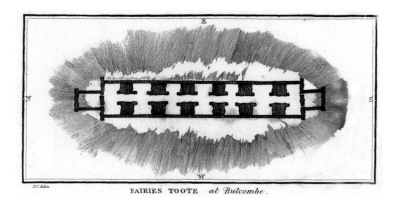

FAIRIES TOOTE *at Butcombe.*

Figure 36: Samuel Seyer's 1821 ground plan of Fairy's Toot

from the reality more complicated. An early example occurs in *The History and Antiquities of the County of Somerset*, published by John Collinson in 1791, where the Toot is described as follows:

"there is a barrow measuring 60 yards [55m] long by 20 yds [18m] in breath and 15 yds [14m] in height, and covered on its top with ash trees, briars and shrubs. On opening it some time ago, its composition throughout was found to be a mass of stones… [with a] series of cells, or cavities, formed by very large stones set edgewise.. and covered with others still larger by way of architrave… in one [cell] were found seven skulls, one quite perfect; in another a vast heap of small human bones and horses teeth. All the cells are not yet opened; and .. no coins or any other relics have been found".[25]

Collinson's account appears to be taken directly from Bere, but there are two additional details. First he states that horses teeth were found. In Bere's account there is mention made of finding "the tooth of some large beast" but why Collinson says that horses' teeth were found is not clear. There is a local story in Nempnett Thrubwell that a horse is buried in a round barrow in the north of the parish[26] and Collinson may have confused this tale. This account of horses' teeth in Fairy's Toot was then repeated elsewhere, for example in the Post Office Directory of Somersetshire and Bristol of 1897. The basis for the very exact figure of seven skulls in one cist is not reported, although this is consistent with Skinner's record of local accounts that many skulls had been found in the Toot.

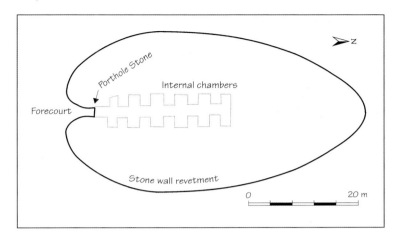

Porthole Stone

Internal chambers

Forecourt

Stone wall revetment

0   20 m

Figure 37: Postulated "true" ground plan of Fairy's Toot

In 1821 Reverend Samuel Seyer published his *Memoirs Historical and Topographical of Bristol and its Neighbourhood*, which includes details of Fairy's Toot, noting its extreme similarity to Stoney Littleton. Seyer appears to have been the first to refer to the barrow as being "at Butcombe." Seyer provides a diagram, which is reproduced in Figure 36, that shows seven pairs of cists running the entire length of the barrow. Seyer gives no details of where the plan came from, but it is very similar to Skinner's 1822 plan (Figure 34). However, Skinner appears not to have approved. Writing in an addition to his 1820 diary (which must have be written after 1828 since it mentions a trip he made in that year to Carnac), Skinner says "Mr. Seyer in his History of Bristol gives a print of it [Fairy's Toot] in more perfect scale but he certainly was mistaken as to the positioning of the cists". [27] What Skinner thinks is wrong with the positioning he does not say.

In John Rutter's 1829 *The Delineations of Somersetshire* he refers to "a remarkable tumulus, called Butcombe Barrow or Fairy's Tout [sic]" so adding to the confusion as to the correct parish. His account of the tumulus is largely a summary of Bere but there are one or two additions. He says of the inside of the barrow "the cells are conjectured to amount to ten or eleven on each side of the avenue", the largest estimate of the number of cists. He accurately records the finds of bones noted by Bere and adds that the mysterious animal teeth are "probably of the red deer", a suggestion in accord with recent work that has shown that red deer were important in the Neolithic economy.

CONCLUSION

It is easy to see why later authors described the accounts of the discovery of Fairy's Toot as "vague and often contradictory." In the space of 40 years the number of pairs of cists inside the barrow was reported as: unknown, possibly eight, probably five or six, and ten or eleven. The amount of detail on the number and location of human skeletons varies considerably. And unidentified animal remains are referred to as those of a large beast, a horse or a red deer. Often it is impossible to tell whether "details" have been derived from actual observation or hearsay.

Notwithstanding these reservations, it is interesting to speculate on the original plan of Fairy's Toot. A careful examination of the work of Bere and Skinner, combined with what has been discovered since about this type of Cotswold Severn tomb, suggests a possible interpretation. Both Bere and Skinner seem convinced there were six or so pairs of chambers, and, given that the barrow was almost twice the size of Stoney Littleton, this seems reasonable (since Stoney Littleton has three pairs). What is less likely is that these chambers would have extended throughout the length of the barrow, and indeed six pairs of cists can be accommodated into a length of 20m, about half the length of Fairy's Toot. It seems likely that the true layout of the Toot would be like that shown in Figure 37: six or so pairs of cists, running about half the length of the barrow.

There remain many unanswered questions about the Toot. Where did the human remains found within go? Were any of the large stones from the tumulus specially kept? Do the fairies still live there? Probably we will never know all the answers, but the Toot is proof that people were living in the parish of Nempnett Thrubwell over 5,000 years ago, and built a monument of some substance and beauty. Anyone interested in understanding what Fairy's Toot would have been like all those years ago should visit Stoney Littleton, which still stands as a reminder of the activities of our ancient predecessors.

4 Place-names

INTRODUCTION

The place-names of England are a source of endless interest and fascination. Nempnett Thrubwell is a classic example, which regularly features in lists of unusual village names, and is the source of many enquiries as to its meaning. But place-names also contain much valuable historical information, and the academic study of English place-names has a long tradition. The main centre for such study is The English Place-Name Society, founded in 1923 with the approval and encouragement of The British Academy, and now located at the University of Nottingham, which published its first major review of place-names in 1924.

In north Somerset the study of place-names is especially important in an understanding of the period between the departure of the Romans in *c.* 410 and the arrival of the Normans in 1066. Over this period there is very little archaeological or written evidence, but Michael Costen, the co-ordinator for the English Place-Name Society survey for Somerset, has shown how a careful study of the names available to us today can throw light on the history of settlement in this period.

The area of the Chew and Yeo valleys is thought to have been well settled and prosperous in Roman times (see Chapter 2), and it appears to have been continued to be have occupied by the native British (or Welsh) to the 7th century. Some Welsh and Celtic names survive today, particularly for major places, rivers and hills; examples include the River Avon, from the early Welsh word meaning river, the River Chew, from the early Welsh word *ciw* (meaning "the young of an animal", quite common as a Welsh river name), and Churchill from *cryc* meaning steep hill.

The Welsh lost political control to the English some time in the 7th century and many English names date from this period; examples include: the many Stokes, from the Old English *stoc* meaning dependent farm, the Wicks, from *wic* "dairy or specialist farm", and two neighbouring parishes which are based on personal names, Ubley being Ubba's ley, that is Ubba's clearing, and Butcombe, previously spelt Budicombe, being Buda's coombe. Michael Costen also finds many examples of Old English names for minor place-names which leads him to conclude that the area was quite densely settled, and that most sites that are settled today were occupied by the 10th century.

Against this general background of the likely pattern of settlement in the north Somerset area over the period 410-1066, the aim of this chapter is to summarise what is known about the origins and meanings of the place-names within Nempnett Thrubwell parish. (A full analysis of field-names is covered in the next chapter.) It should be stressed that this task is not straightforward and it is unrealistic to expect a consensus on every place-name, and sometimes there are two reasonable hypotheses for the meaning of a name. Of particular importance is the way the spelling of place-names changes over time. Thus the spelling in early references is of particular importance, and tracking down such early references is an important part of the search for the meaning of place-names.

The earliest written evidence of place-names for most English parishes comes from Saxon documents, which are few and far between, and the Domesday Book. For the medieval period and later, there are many legal and ecclesiastical records that may provide important data. Thus for Nempnett the records of the Manor of Regilbury, which date back in reasonably accessible form to about 1700, are of particular importance.

Maps are critical too. For place- and field-names in Nempnett the most important source is the Tithe Map and Apportionment of 1841, which provides a detailed parish map with every field named. There appear to be only two detailed maps that predate the Tithe Map. There is a plan and valuation of Regilbury Court, Regilbury Park Farm, and the nearby Crudwells Tenement, dated 1778, which gives field names for some areas in the north-east of the parish, see Plate 16.[1] Second, there is a set of maps dated 1794-1811 of the lands of Isaac Elton Esq. in Nempnett which cover a part of the south of the parish but on which there are very few place- or field-names, see Plate 19.[2]

In addition three early maps which cover a wider area are considered in detail, namely Donne's 1742 map of Bristol and surrounds, the 1782 Day and Masters' map of Somerset, and Greenwood's 1822 map of Somerset; all three of these maps contain some useful information on the parish of Nempnett.

NEMPNETT THRUBWELL

First the parish name, Nempnett Thrubwell – what does it mean? And where does it come from? It is clear from early records that the names Nempnett and Thrubwell originally referred to separate places. Nempnett appears to have been used first for the area around the church, and later for the parish as a whole. The name Thrubwell was used from early times separately, to refer to a farm or manor in the north of the parish, it is thought at or near today's Thrubwell Farm. There are also occasional references to the Tithing of Thrubwell, for example in the 1569 Certificate of Musters and on the Butcombe Tithe map, although the relationship between this tithing and the parish is not clear. It is not until some time in the 19th century that the "joint" name of Nempnett Thrubwell was adopted for the parish.

These historical facts mean that any attempt to explain the name Nempnett Thrubwell as a single entity is incorrect. For example, Robinson's 1992 *Somerset Place-names* says the name means "the grove at the village well" from the Celtic *nemett* (grove) and the Old English *prop wiell* (village well) but this must be wrong. A less-serious suggestion, but it might be right you never know, is given by Douglas Adams: Nempnett Thrubwell "the feeling experienced when driving off for the first time on a brand new motorbike". But for a more likely explanation we need to consider the names separately.

Nempnett

There are no references to the place-name Nempnett in the Domesday Book, but this is of no especial significance since Domesday was concerned with manors and land ownership rather than all places - about 80 present-day Somerset parishes are not mentioned in the Domesday text.[3] Nor is there any surviving Saxon charter for Nempnett, or for any of the neighbouring parishes (the nearest being the Wrington charter of 904).

The first written records of Nempnett appear around 1200 where the usual spelling in Emnet.

> In 1208 in the Curia Regis Rolls, the written record of the Kings' Courts, there is a dispute between Hugo Hose and the Abbot of Flaxley "concerning four virgates [about 120 acres of land] with appurtenances in Emnet".[4]

> The Cartulary and Historical Notes of the Cistercian Abbey of Flaxley, thought to have been written in the time of King John between 1199 and 1216, contains a number of references to Emnet. For example there is "the gift of Hugh Hosate of all his land at Emmett with appurtenances"; there is a reference to "two acres of Emnet" in a grant from Walter Sprot of Ragel [Regilbury]; the church of "Emnet" receives a yearly payment from the Abbey; and Godfrey Chaplain of Emnet appears as a witness to many grants and deeds to the abbey.[5]

> The Calendar of the Manuscripts of the Dean and Chapter of Wells contains a record of an indenture of agreement made in 1242 between Sir John Bretasche [of Thrubwell] and the Rector of Compton Martin, which includes reference to "the church of Empnete which is a chapel of the mother church of Compton [Martin]."[6]

Later references use all sorts of spellings including Nemett, Nemnet, Nymet, Nimet, Nemlet, Emet, and Nympnet, so that it is perhaps not surprising there are many theories about the meaning of Nempnett. However, amongst place-name scholars the favoured explanation is that given by Professor Eilert Ekwall, an early member of the English Place-Name Society, whose work is still held in high regard. In his *The Concise Oxford Dictionary of English Place-Names* first published in 1947, Ekwall states that the name Nempnett is derived from the Old English word *emnet* meaning "a plain, a plateau or level ground", with the prefix N- deriving from the Middle English word *atten* meaning "at the", so the name means "on or of the plain/plateau" or "place at the level ground."

At first meeting this explanation may seem inappropriate, since the parish as a whole is distinctly hilly. But the name may not have originally applied to the whole parish, merely a part of it that was flat: "the proximity of hills is precisely the reason for a place on flat ground to be distinctive – the name originally has no necessary connection to the whole parish".

To explore this idea further a classification of slopes in the parish was derived, and the results are shown in Figure 38. The degree of slope is classified into one of four types, the steepest slopes being in black, quite steeply sloping land in dark grey, slightly sloping in light grey and relatively level land in white. [7] The map shows that steeply sloping land is common in the southern half of the parish, and to the north, east and south of the church (some of it outside the parish boundary). If the name Nempnett originally applied to the church and the area immediately adjacent, especially to the west, then this area is indeed flat compared with the land all around (as shown by the white area on the map to the west of the church). One can imagine an early visitor to the church commenting on the pleasant level nature of the place, especially compared to the hills just climbed.

There are, however, alternative explanations. The Rev James Hill's *Place-names of Somerset* published in 1914 suggests the name means "Empa's headland," a combination of the personal name Emp and the ending -et that is a reduced form of the Old English *heafod* meaning headland. This makes sense in a topographic sense if the name applied originally to the area near the church, since there are striking views from the churchyard to the north and east as from a headland.

Another possibility is that the name dates from the earlier period of pre-English settlement and derives from the Welsh *nemet* or *nemeton* meaning a holy place. This might be appropriate if the name applied to the area around the church which may well have been a holy site before the Christian church was built there. The argument would be that later this word changed to the English *atten emnet* and that by the time written records appear in the 13th century the *nemet* spelling had been lost or forgotten.

The balance of opinion amongst place-name scholars, however, is that Ekwall's explanation is the most likely to be correct. If the name really came from *heafod,* as Hill suggests, early spellings would probably include endings in -ed or -head, which is not the case, and the vast majority of names which are thought to have been derived from *heafod* today end in -head. And if the name came from *nemet* then early spellings would be expected to have an N- at the front and not to have the -m(p)n- in the middle. Ekwall's explanation is also preferred because it is a "simplex" explanation, that is to say one which depends upon a single word *emnet*, and also because his work is now held in higher esteem than that of Hill.

Thrubwell

The first references to the place-name Thrubwell also appear around 1200, with spellings that vary but are all quite close to the modern day version.

> In the Assize Rolls for Somerset of 1201 there is a dispute involving the Bretasche family over "twelve acres of wood, with the appurtenances in Trubewel".[8]

> In the Feet of Fines for Somerset of 1239 there is another dispute involving the Bretasche family over "common pasture in Trubewelle".[9]

> An indenture between Sir John Bretasche and the Rector of Compton recorded in The Calendar of the Manuscripts of the Dean and Chapter of Wells in 1242 describes a "chapel erected by the said Sir John in his court of Trubbewell".[10]

> In the Cartulary of Flaxley there is a record dated *c.* 1227 that Peter de Salso Mariso (Peter of Salt Marsh) "gave to the monks all his land in Tribnell with all appurtenances" (although in another entry the spelling is Tribnelle).[11]

The accepted explanation of Thrubwell is that the "Thrub" component means gushing or bubbling from OE *thrybb* related to modern English throb and that "well" means spring or well (usually in place-names a natural spring) so that the name means "by a gushing spring or well". The name originally seems to have applied to a manor in the north of the parish, probably at or close to Thrubwell Farm (see Chapter 9). Since there are many springs and wells close to Thrubwell Farm this explanation is consistent with the local setting. The occasional references to the Tithing of Thrubwell, including its appearance on the Butcombe Tithe Map, are also consistent with this location.

One intriguing question remains however. John Rutter in his discussion of Thrubwell Manor says it "derived its name from a spring called Thrub-well, formerly of some notoriety"[12] but

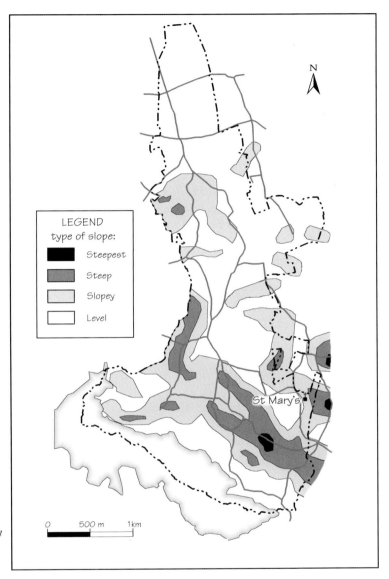

FIgure 38: Classification of slopes in Nempnett Thrubwell

he gives no indication as to what form this notoriety took! Phil Quinn in his book *Holy Wells of Bath and Bristol Region* notes that there was often merry-making around holy wells as certain times of year, notably May Day, and suggests that Thrubwell's notoriety might be due to such festivities becoming somewhat unruly (although Phil Quinn presents no direct evidence that Thrubwell was a holy well).

MINOR PLACE-NAMES: FARMS AND HOUSES

This section draws together what is known about the names of various farms and houses within the parish, where these are thought to be related to places. The emphasis here is on names that date back to at least the 18th century. It should be emphasised that this is a discussion of the place-names, their age and likely meaning, not of the buildings now standing.

Belvedere Manor, the name of the dwelling immediately adjacent to the church, is a relatively recent name, which appears about 1900. It is probably from the French *bel videre* "beautiful view", an appropriate name. Before that the name is Glebe Farm (see for example the first edition Ordnance Survey map of *c.* 1888) indicating its association with the church.

Bicknell Farm is close to a small hill reaching about 165m above sea level, a spot from which there are outstanding views in all directions, and which is known to have been settled since pre-historic times (see Chapter 2). The name Bicknell is thought to mean "Pointed Hill," the prefix derived from Old English *bican* or *bickn* meaning point, or beak shaped, the suffix from the Old English word *hyll* or *ell* "hill".

The name appears to be old, since an early reference appears in a deed of 1314 between Joan Bretasche [of Thrubwell Manor] and the master of the hospital of St. John the Baptist of Redcliffe, Bristol, where there is reference to "three perches of land in Budicome [Butcombe] lying in a field called Garstone under Bikenhulle".[13] The deed is in Latin and Bikenhulle is textbook Middle English for the Old English elements *bican* or *bickn* and *hyll* or *ell* mentioned above. The two fields immediately south of the hill next to Bicknell Farm, which lie in Butcombe Parish, are named Garstons in the 1841 Tithe Map, suggesting that the name Bickenhulle does apply to the place we now call Bicknell.

Cuckoo's Nest dates back as a name to at least 1730, when it appears in a survey of the lands of the Manor of Regilbury; at that time it appears to have referred to a cottage and a small strip of land, and was occupied by Richard West, who also lived there back to 1714.[14] The name also appears on the map of Isaac Elton's lands in the parish, which dates to *c.* 1811, see Plate 19. Whether the name then refers to a specific house, or an area, is not clear. The origin of the name probably alludes to cuckoos, perhaps a close or wood used by them. There are many other place-names in the parish associated with birds.

Henmarsh Farm. To follow Margaret Gelling the name Henmarsh is likely to mean "wild birds' marsh." Like its neighbour Rugmoor Farm, this derives from the time when the area in the south of the parish near the River Yeo was poorly drained and marshy.

Howgrove Farm. The first reference to this place-name is in 1239 in a dispute between John Bretasche, of Thrubwell Manor, and Brother Roger, Master of the Hospital of St. John the Baptist, Redcliffe, Bristol, over "common of pasture in Trubewelle... in the wood called Hugrave".[15] Later references include deeds of 1795 where the spelling is Huggrove,[16] the 1782 Day and Masters' Map of Somerset (figure 41) where the name appears as Hygrove, and the 1822 Greenwoods Map of Somerset (figure 42), spelt there as High Grove. By the time of the Tithe Map in 1841 the spelling Howgrove had been adopted.

On the basis of this information a likely derivation is that the first component comes from the Old English *hoh*, meaning "heel", in the sense of "a sharply projecting piece of ground", and the second component from the Old English *graf* "grove" or "copse". Although the current Howgrove Farm is more in a valley location than a hill spur, it may have taken its name from a nearby place.

Merry Hill Farm. In 18th century documents of the Manor of Regilbury this name appears as Merry Fields, Merefields, and Merefields Hill.[17] There are two possible explanations of the name. First, the place-name Merryfields may mean "pleasant open land," with merry derived from the Old English *myrig* "merry", a name that is particularly common in Devon, and field from the Old English *feld* "open country". Alternatively, the early spellings suggest the name may come originally from the OE *mere* meaning a pond or lake. In this particular case the name seems to have started as Merryfields or Merefields, then become Merryfields Hill and then finally Merry Hill.

Pixey Hall Farm. The history of this name is complicated. The hall component is said by Margaret Gelling to often be derived from the Old English *halh* "nook" or *holh* "hollow," to indicate a sunken place and 19th century spellings suggest this is the case here, since the name is Pixey Hole in the first edition Ordnance Survey map of 1888 and in the census returns of 1841-91. The Pixey part may not be the earliest spelling either, since the 1730 survey of the Manor of Regilbury has a Pigg Stie Hole and a Pigg Stie Cottage,[18] but it is easy to see why later residents might have preferred an alternative, and rather more appealing, spelling.

Regilbury has a long history as a place-name. Today there is Regilbury Court and Regilbury Park Farm, but previously there was Regilbury Manor. The name is the only one from the parish to feature in the Domesday Book, where it is spelt Ragiol. In the Cartulary of Flaxley *c.* 1200 there are references to Ragel, Ragelbury and Rachelbury.[19] In the documents concerning the dissolution of Flaxley Abbey dated 1537-44 it is spelt Rochelbury or Rothelbury. After this it is generally known as the Manor of Regelbury or Regilbury, and other similar variants.

There two main theories of the meaning of Regilbury. The first, as suggested by Professor Ekwall, is that the name means "the fortified manor-house at or by the roe-deer hill escarpment". The first part comes from the Old English *ra* "roe-deer" and *ecg* "an edge" which is usually taken to mean an escarpment (although an alternative interpretation of *ecg* is that it refers to a place near a boundary, usually an administrative boundary), so that we have *ra-ecg* "roe-deer escarpment"; the second element is plausibly *hyll* "hill." The -bury derives from Old English *burh*, but it is not present in the earliest form Ragiol, suggesting the meaning "fortified manor-house."

An alternative explanation, given in the recent *Cambridge Dictionary of English Place-Names* (2004) is that the Regil component of the name the name derives from the Cornish dialect *radgell* "an excavated tunnel, or a number of stones lying about". A possible basis for a "number of stones lying about" is the tor-like feature at ST52886352, some 600m to the NNW of Regilbury Court Farm, an assemblage of rock rather like a Dartmoor tor, but on a smaller scale and on a slope; the largest stones measure about 2m high by 3m wide and are surrounded by a number of smaller boulders "lying around". This feature is hidden by trees and on private land, but there is a collection of similar but smaller boulders on the east side of Hen Lane at ST52876358. The "excavated tunnel" explanation is of note given the local legend of a tunnel between Regilbury and Butcombe Court.

There is one other theory that is worth mentioning, although it is incorrect. The Reverend John Skinner visited Regilbury, which he spelled Regelsbury, in 1822 and he says of it in his diary "the name seems to imply a royal residence in the Saxon times".[20] But as Skinner seems to be suggesting a derivation from the Latin for king *rex*, or *regis*, this is not a plausible explanation.

Rugmoor Farm. The component moor is from the Old English *mor*, which is used in two ways: for a barren upland area, as for example in Dartmoor and Exmoor, or for low-lying marshes, such as in Sedgemoor and Wedmore. In the present case it is the latter use that makes more sense, since Rugmoor Farm is in the low-lying area of the parish close to the River Yeo, which would have been heavy marshy land until properly drained. The prefix rug is likely to be from OE *ruh* meaning rough or uncultivated. An alternative is that rug is a Modern English dialect term meaning "land covered in large stones" but it seems likely that the name is older than that.

Yeo (the river) is probably from the OE *ea* meaning river, a common name in Somerset and Devon.

MINOR PLACE-NAMES: HILLS AND RIDGES

The Tithe Map of 1841 provides a complete survey of field names in the parish, and a full analysis of these names is considered in Chapter 5. Here the focus is on those names in the Tithe Map and earlier sources that refer to hills or high places. Many of these names have been lost, and few are in everyday use, but they are part of the history of the parish and deserve to be more widely known and used. The place-names discussed in this section are shown in Figure 39.

Kingdown. The high land at the very north of the parish is often referred to as Kingdown or Kingsdown Hill or Common in early documents. The name appears to date back to at least the beginning of the 18th century since an entry in Florence Baber's will of 1711 refers to "my Kings lands in Nempnett", and there are many references in the 18th and 19th century documents of Regilbury Manor to "lands on Kingsdown Hill or Common in Nempnett".[21] The origins of this name are not clear, but the fact that this area was probably owned by Flaxley Abbey over the period *c.* 1200-1536, and that the Abbey had royal connections (see Chapter 6), may provide an explanation.

Whitestone Hill appears as the name of a field just south of Thrubwell Farm in the Tithe Map, although it is not certain the "hill" refers to a landscape feature. A likely explanation for the "whitestone" part of the name is that this was the site of mining for strontia, a white stone, chemically one of the alkaline earths, which is known to have been mined in this area around the end of the 19th century.[22] The "hill" might refer to a minor landscape feature, or possibly to an old spoil heap.

Honey Mead Hill is close to Regilbury Court, a charming name dating back to at least 1778, when it was recorded on a plan and valuation of Regilbury Court, Park Farm and Crudwells Tenement (see Plate 16).[23] The mead part comes from OE/ME *mæd* meaning a meadow or grassland, while the honey part may refer to the high productivity of the land (as in "flowing with milk and honey"), the colour of the soil, the sticky nature of the soil, a place where wild honey could be found or a place where bees were kept.

Rooks (Hooks) Hill. On the western edges of the parish is a group of fields called Hooks Hill in the Tithe Map, which lie on the high land to the west of Nempnett Farm. However, earlier references in documents of the Manor of Regilbury holdings use the name Rooks Hill.[24] Since Rooks Hill is the earlier spelling, it seems better to use this name. Certainly there are many other examples of places in the parish named after birds, and it may be that the change from Rook to Hook came about by misspelling. There is no obvious explanation of the alternative name Hooks Hill.

Bosmead Hill. To the north-east of Nempnett Farm there is a small hill called Bosmead in the Tithe Map. A possible explanation is that this derives from an Old English personal name, so that Bosmead means "Bosa's meadow".

Ashills. On the eastern edge of the parish, on the high land to the south of Bosmead Hill and north of the church, a series of fields in the Tithe Map have the name Ashills, including Ashills Paddock and Ashills Wood. The same name occurs in a document of 1770 concerning the Estates of Thomas Prowse, where there is reference to Ashills Wood in Nempnett.[25] This name is thought to mean Ash-tree Hill.

Chickey or Chitty Hill (see Plate 6). The high ground immediately to the north-east of West Town is known as Chitty Hill in the Tithe Map, where this field-name occurs six times. However, in earlier documents of Regilbury Manor the name is Chickey Hill,[26] so that Chitty may be a later version. The derivation of Chickey is not clear. It might come from the growing of chicory, or possibly from the Primitive Welsh *ced* meaning wood which is the basis for Chicklade and Chitterne in Wiltshire. Although no longer wooded, the area is likely to have remained wooded until maybe the 14th century (see Chapter 5).

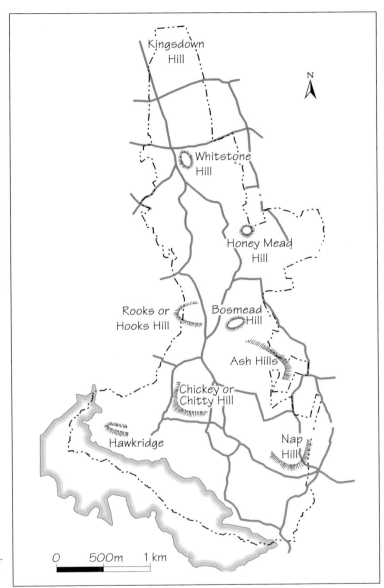

Figure 39: The hills of Nempnett Thrubwell

Nap Hill is the name used in the Tithe Map for the very steep hill to the south of the church. As mentioned above, The Rev Hill suggested this is Empa's Hill. An alternative and probably more accurate explanation is that it is derived from the Old English *cnæpp* meaning hilltop or a short sharp ascent so that Knap or Nap Hill would mean a very steep hill, an accurate description.

Hawkridge. Finally, the very steep ridge in the south-west of the parish, a prominent landscape feature of the hard Butcombe Sandstone overlooking Blagdon Lake, which has a Bronze Age barrow at its end, has the name Hawkridge in the Tithe Map (see Chapter 2, Figure 8, and Plate 6).

EARLY MAPS

In 1742 John Donne published his circular map of Bristol and the surrounding area, and part of his map for the area around Nempnett is shown in Figure 40. The map is incomplete, for example no roads are shown in the central part of the parish, but there are several points of interest. The name Nempnet is used for the area around the church, but the name Thrubwell does not appear. To the north of the parish the name King's Down appears. A number of properties are identified by their owner or occupier. For example, Mr. Sommers appears by Thrubwell Farm and Mr. Curtis by Butcombe Court (see Chapter 8). Regilbury appears as Regilsbury Farm with the name Sir C K Tynte (see Chapter 7).

An extract of the Day and Masters map of Somerset of 1782 is shown in Figure 41. This map is more complete in terms of the roads and settlement of the village. The name Nemnet appears by the church and there is also Nemnet Farm. West Town is shown as a separate hamlet, and to the north there is Hygrove (Howgrove Farm). The name Regilbury Park appears by two buildings, although it is not clear if this is a single name, or if Regilbury applies to the northern building and Park to the other. Longthorn Lane is shown as of equivalent importance to other lanes in the parish and has a number of buildings along it.

An extract of the Greenwood map of Somerset of 1882 is shown in Figure 42. Now there is the name Nempnet by the church, and Nempnet Farm. Just north of Nempnet Farm the dark irregular patch is Ashills Wood. At Regilbury there are the separate entries of Regilbury Court and Regilbury Park. Just north-east of this the name Long Thorn is used to suggest a small hamlet along Long Thorn Lane. This is the only known occurrence of Long Thorn as a place-name, and its likely meaning is "the place by the large hawthorn-tree"; it is interesting that in place-names thorn trees are often associated with boundaries. West Town is again shown again as a separate hamlet, with Howgrove Farm

Figure 40: Extract from John Donne's 1742 map of Bristol and surrounds

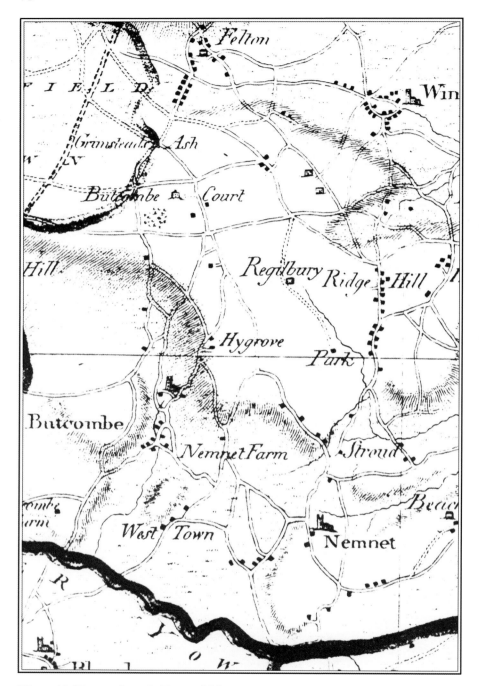

Figure 41: Extract from the Day and Masters 1782 map of Somerset

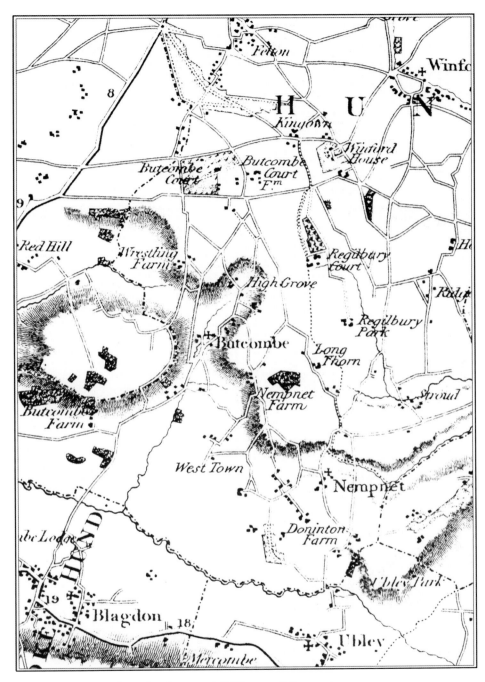

Figure 42: Extract from the Greenwood 1822 map of Somerset

now spelt High Grove. Thrubwell Farm appears to be called Butcombe Court Farm.

CONCLUSIONS

Many place-names now strike us as unusual, quaint or just downright odd, but as Michael Costen has written "somewhere in the past all place-names had an obvious and easy meaning. It is the passage of time and the inevitable changes of language which have made the names obscure to us".[27]   This chapter has aimed to explore the meanings of certain place-names in the parish, and to bring to light again some names that are no longer in general use.

As well as their intrinsic interest, place-names "also carry a great deal of historical information if we can read them right",[28] and if the analysis of this chapter is correct it suggests that the parish was fairly densely inhabited by the 10th century, since many minor place-names have Old English derivations.

One specific topic to arise here is the suggestion that there was once a hamlet called Long Thorn on the eastern boundaries of the parish centred on Long Thorn Lane. The possibility that Long Thorn is a deserted or abandoned settlement will be looked at again in later chapters.

5   Fields and Field-names

INTRODUCTION

Fields have been part of the English landscape since the early days of agriculture, and the earliest fields probably date back 5,000 years. Since then fields have been central to the cultivation of the land, providing a way of organising arable land and controlling domestic animals. Over the centuries farming practices have changed, and so have fields and field systems, so that a careful analysis of existing field patterns, or the patterns recorded at earlier dates on maps, can provide important information on local history. An excellent introductory book is *Fields in the English Landscape* by Christopher Taylor (1975).

It is likely that there have been field-names for as long as there have been fields, because names provide a simple and practical method for referring to a particular piece of land. Many of these names are descriptive of such everyday matters as the quality of the soil, the shape of the field, or the crops grown, but other names may refer to the history of the field or to features of archaeological interest. In some cases these field-names may be the only remaining evidence of features that have disappeared. Like place-names, field-names once had an obvious and easy meaning, which may be uncovered by careful study.

The most importance source for the historical study of fields and field-names in Nempnett Thrubwell is the Tithe Map and Apportionment of 1841, which includes a detailed map of the parish on which every field is mapped and named. There are some scattered earlier references to fields and field-names in earlier documents, especially those of the Manor of Regilbury, but these references rarely contain maps so it is only by careful cross-referencing to the Tithe Map that their location can be identified.

THE FIELDS OF THE TITHE MAP

The fields of Nempnett Thrubwell as recorded in 1841 are shown in Figure 43. Because of changes in the parish boundary and the way the Tithe Maps were collected the information on this map is in fact derived from three sources: the Tithe Map for Nempnett Thrubwell, the Tithe Map for Winford (for the area around Henmarsh Farm then in the parish of Winford – see Chapter 1 and Figure 3), and the separate Tithe Map for the land belonging to Sir Charles Kemeys Kemeys-Tynte (for the area around Regilbury Court and Regilbury Park Farm). In Figure 43 dashed lines indicate boundaries between pieces of land in different ownership where there is no physical boundary on the ground.

In broad terms Nempnett Thrubwell appears to form part of what Oliver Rackham calls the "Ancient Countryside of Lowland Britain",[1] the major features of which are: settlement in the form of very small hamlets and ancient, isolated farmsteads; fields which are small and usually irregular in shape; and deeply incised, narrow and winding lanes. In these ancient landscapes most fields date to the medieval period or earlier.

On the basis of the size and shape of the fields recorded in the Tithe Map, and using documentary sources where available, the parish may be divided into seven sub-areas to reflect differences in the history of the field systems, as shown in Figure 43. The main source for this analysis is the Avon Historic Landscape Characterisation project undertaken in 1995-98; this project was county-wide so the boundaries are likely to be approximate. These seven areas are now discussed in turn.

Area 1: Kingsdown Common: 18th Century Enclosure
An area of about 100 acres at the very north of the parish on the high land usually referred to as Kingsdown Hill (or previously Kingsdown Common), contains regularly-shaped fields of around 6-10 acres in size, the distinctive shape and size of 18th or 19th century enclosures. Christopher Taylor describes this pattern as showing "the rigid geometry... of the hand of the professional

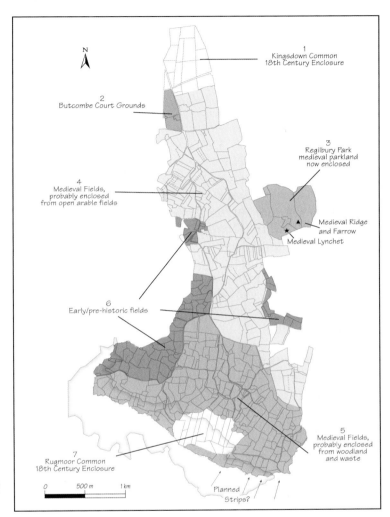

N

1
Kingsdown Common
18th Century Enclosure

2
Butcombe Court Grounds

3
Regilbury Park
medieval parkland
now enclosed

4
Medieval Fields,
probably enclosed
from open arable fields

Medieval Ridge
and Farrow
Medieval Lynchet

6
Early/pre-historic fields

5
Medieval Fields,
probably enclosed
from woodland
and waste

7
Rugmoor Common
18th Century Enclosure

0   500 m   1 km

Planned
Strips?

Figure 43: Fields of the Tithe Map 1841 classified by likely field origin

surveyor who planned these fields", an accurate description of their genesis. This area was probably unfenced common land for summer grazing until it was enclosed some time in the late 18th century. Unusually, there appear to be no records of this enclosure. The book by W C Tate *Somerset Enclosure Acts and Awards* (1948) has no entries for Nempnett but there are records of enclosures in Wrington parish on Wrington Hill and Broadfield Down in 1810-1815. The road which runs east-west to the south of this block of land is called "New Road" suggesting it may have been constructed at the time of enclosure and post-dates other lanes in the area.

Area 2: Butcombe Court grounds

A small area of *c.* 20 acres of the parish is part of the Butcombe Court grounds. This is a formal post-medieval designed ornamental landscape, with the magnificent lime trees lined along the drive, quite different from the remainder of the parish — see Plate 7.

Area 3: Regilbury Park

A second area with a history of a formally designed landscape is to be found around Regilbury Park Farm. The fields here, whose names include Home Park, Further Park, Park Gate Paddock and Pond Mead, are post-medieval created from the enclosure of medieval parkland.

The most obvious features of a medieval park were its boundary and shape. The boundaries were expensive to erect and maintain so parks tended to be oval or circular in shape, as is the case here. The boundary itself may have once been a considerable bank, possibly topped with a wooden fence. Regilbury Park measures roughly 100 acres, at the small end in terms of size, most local parks measuring between 100 and 150 acres. The main use of the park was to hunt deer, but the smaller ones have been described as "little more than venison larders". More than 40 parks were created in the County of Avon in the medieval period, the nearest being Ubley Park which adjoins the south-east corner of the parish.[2]

Nick Balmer, a historian of the Baber family, has suggested that Regilbury Park was planned by Sir Christopher Hatton, who also designed and built Holdenby near Althorp in 1583, but I have no further details of this.

The area of Regilbury Park also contains the only recorded examples of medieval ridge and furrow and medieval lynchets in the parish. Just to the south and east of Regilbury Park Farm are two sites in the Sites and Monuments Record referring to early medieval arable cultivation. To the south "a set of low, heavily ploughed lynchets, mostly less than 1m high" aligned NW-SE have been noted and mapped on the SMR records (SMR 6275). Lynchets are small ridges formed as the result of ploughing on sloping ground in medieval or earlier times.

To the east of Regilbury Park farm are "a set of linear features aligned WNW-ESE.. [being] earthworks of a fairly well preserved ridge and furrow, width 16m, running downhill to within *c.* 20m of the stream. Low banks to the north *c.* 5m wide and 0.5m

Figure 44: Aerial photograph of Regilbury Park Farm showing evidence of medieval lynchets and ridge and furrow

high, one lying along the contour and one perpendicular to it are almost certainly old field boundaries" (SMR 6276). Ridge and furrow is a product of medieval ploughing very similar in form to lynchets.[3]

An extract from an aerial photograph taken in January 1946 of this area is shown in Figure 44.[4] The buildings of Regilbury Park Farm are in the top centre of the picture. The lynchets are just apparent as pale, linear stripes running NW-SE in the field immediately to the south, and the ridge and furrow as similar features running almost E-W in the field to the east. Both these sites were recorded by local archaeologists in 1989. It is possible that the creation of a park in medieval times helped preserve these features.

Area 4: Medieval fields, probably enclosed from open arable fields
Most of the northern part of the parish, the area of high and relatively flat ground, is classified in this category, although it is likely that there are variations within the area. The fields here are typically small and regular in outline, following the lay of the land, but interrupted by the winding lanes and lacking the regularity of the 18th and 19th century enclosures. The overall pattern is a hotchpotch of small fields reflecting the fact that they developed over a long period of time, rather than being planned "at a stroke".

This area is one where settlement and farming has a very long history; for example, chapter 2 has noted the evidence of Romano-British settlement near Bicknell Farm. It is likely that this area would have been the preferred area for settlement within the parish in Anglo-Saxon times and the early medieval period: Kingsdown Common would have been too high (too cold), the hilly land just to the south too difficult to cultivate, and the very south of the parish by the River Yeo too damp.

A typical form of Anglo-Saxon settlement would have been of small hamlets surrounded by a field system of "in-fields" and "out-fields". The in-fields close to the settlement would have been intensively cultivated, mainly for arable crops like wheat and barley. These fields required a lot of labour, and used manure from domestic stock housed near the farm in winter, so being close to the farmstead was an advantage. The "out-fields", further from the farmstead, would have been cultivated less intensively, and provided seasonal crops like hay, summer grazing, and wood.

In the early medieval period what are known as "open-fields" developed, although there is much debate about the timing and reasons for this, and open-fields vary greatly across the country. The common characteristic is that fields were managed communally. Individuals owned, or leased, "strips" of land which were scattered throughout the open field or fields, to ensure fairness (a roughly equal share of good and bad land). These strips were of any length but typically 10-20m wide, and were cultivated by ploughs drawn by 6 or 8 oxen. Repeated ploughing of the strips led to ridge-and-furrow patterns, where the central area (the ridge) was raised by the action of the plough turning over the soil, and the resulting furrows served to demarcate strips and to aid drainage.

In many parts of lowland England, especially in the Midlands, very large open-fields surrounded growing villages, but in Nempnett it is likely that the open-fields were always of quite limited extent, associated with very small groups of individuals living in a hamlet. Enclosure of open-fields took place roughly over the period 1400-1700, in a piecemeal way by local arrangements such as the exchange of strips, although "such early enclosure is often poorly documented, and rarely mapped; the best evidence is to be found in the field patterns and the dates of the accompanying farms".[5]

Two areas in the parish where this pattern is particularly marked are near Long Thorn Lane and Bicknell Farm. In both

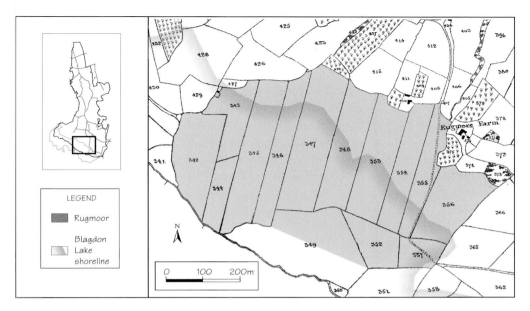

Figure 47: Extract from the 1841 Tithe Map showing the the estimated extent of Rugmoor Common

the property of Francis Mann (who was probably Lord of the Manor of Butcombe Court in the early 18th century).

Independent commissioners were appointed to oversee this process of enclosure, namely Thomas Pippen of Butcombe, Christopher Budge of Chew Stoke and Peter Fry of Axbridge. They were charged with dividing the moor up between those with rights of common in proportion to the size of their existing rights, while taking into account the different quality of the soil of the land, and trying to make the resulting fields as close as possible to the owners' respective farms. It was also noted that the common had traditionally been divided into two parts by large stones, with the western part of the moor allocated to the tenants of Sir Charles Kemeys Kemeys-Tynte and the eastern part to Francis Mann.

The role of these stones, and some dark deeds concerning them, are recorded in an examination of Mary Holbrook, taken on 16 November 1772. Her testimony is as follows:

> Mary Holbrook of Nempnett, widow, saith she was born in the said parish of Nempnett in which parish and in the adjoining parish of Budicombe she have constantly lived.

That she well remembers for upwards of sixty years ago to have often seen two large stones in a certain common field commonly called and known by the name Rug Moor, which said stones she always understood to be Ancient Law Marks, set up as a division or partition for dividing the said Rugmoor between the Lords of the Fee of the said Rugmoor (viz Lords Mann and Baber). That she well remembers one of the stones which was on the north side of the said Rugmoor, a complaint being made to the said Mr. Mann it was not standing upright and the said Mr. Mann went with the examinant's father to the said Moor Stone and ordered him to set it upright in its usual place. That some time after the said Mr. Mann died, and her father neglected to have the said stone putt up. And then this examinant further saith that she remembers about that time her father and William Vowles had a dispute about the said stone on the north side, and soon after the said stone was removed but was not immediately known by whom. That some time after the said William Vowles acknowledged it was he that did it. That she believes the death of Mr. Mann prevented the said William Vowles from being prosecuted for the above offence. That she well remembers the place where the Ancient Bound Stone taken away by the said William Vowles stood, and at the request of certain commissioners nominated for enclosing the said Rugmoor she has now shown the exact place where it stood sixty years since, at which place the commissioners have in my presence and in the presence of others put and placed a stone. That she likewise remembers to have had her father and brother and other old people say upwards of sixty years ago that the place where the above said stone is now put was the exact boundary between the said Mr. Mann and Mr. Baber. And also that she is now informed that the share which did then belong to Mr. Mann is now the property of diverse people, and the share which did then belong to Mr. Baber is now the property of Sir Charles Kemeys Tynte Baronet.[11]

The testimony is signed with the mark of Mary Holbrook, and witnessed by John Vowles and John Dunn.

The allocation which the commissioners made to the 10 people with rights in Rugmoor Common is summarised in Table 1. The first group of six are the tenants of Regilbury Manor; the second

Tenant/Occupier	Place of Residence	Oxen Shutts	Acreage allocated	Description of the location
Thomas Beale	Butcombe	8.5	7-1-19	At the west end of the common
Richard Vowles	Nempnett	6	6-1-38	Adjoining and to the east of Thomas Beale's land
Samuel Vowles	Nempnett	7.5	8-0-18	Adjoining and to the east of Richard Vowles' land
William Bennett	Nempnett	5	5-1-25	Adjoining and to the east of Samuel Vowles' land
Samuel Poole	Blagdon	3	4-0-22	Adjoining and to the east of William Bennett's land
James Hellier	Nempnett	5	7-0-34	Adjoining and to the east of Samuel Poole's land
Samuel Sage	Butcombe	3	6-0-28	Adjoining and to the east of James Hellier's land
Henry Hellier	Nempnett	8	12-1-16	Adjoining and to the east of Samuel Sage's land
Christopher Young	Olveston	11	17-1-21	Adjoining and to the east of Henry Hellier's land
John Cam	Yatton	3.5	5-1-38	Adjoing and to the southwest of Christopher Young's land and to the south of Samuel Sage's land

Table 1: Allocation of land on Rugmoor Common to tenants/occupiers

group of four those who had purchased land from Mr. Mann. The table shows the original rights of common as measured in Oxen Shutts, the new acreage allocated, measured in A-R-P, that is acres, rods, and perches, and a brief description of where the land lay. Further details of these individuals and their farms can be found in Chapters 8 and 9.

Fields of the Tithe Map: Summary

The discussion of these seven sub-areas within the parish shows how the shape and size of fields recorded on the Tithe Map can be used to throw light on the settlement history of the parish. It seems likely that the northern parts of the parish around Regilbury, Bicknell, Howgrove, Long Thorn and (perhaps) Nempnett Farm have the longest history of settlement, probably extending back to early medieval times at least. The slopes to the south and the land near the River Yeo are likely to have been settled later, possibly by 1300, as population and demand for land increased. After these periods of expansion in the medieval period, there appear to have been very few changes to the settlement pattern and landscape, the most notable being the enclosure of Rugmoor and Kingsdown Commons and the apparent disappearance of a settlement, probably a small hamlet, at Long Thorn.

The elongated shape of the parish makes a great deal of sense as an economic unit, since it includes the four key types of land necessary for a successful Anglo-Saxon or early medieval estate: **arable** land on the high flat plateau, **woodland** on the slopes to the south, **meadowland** for hay on the low damp land by Rugmoor, and **pasture** for grazing on the high land of Kingsdown and perhaps after the final hay cut in the meadows.[12] If indeed the parish was such an estate (or estates), its origins may date back to Roman or earlier times, since these early farmers needed the same mix of land uses and later settlers may well have just taken over successful estates.

There are also some areas within the parish that appear to have fields that date back to prehistoric times and possibly Roman times. Although little is known of these fields their presence emphasises the very ancient nature of some of the landscape of the parish, with some of the fields we see and use today being maybe thousands of years old.

THE FIELD-NAMES OF THE TITHE MAP

The Tithe Map of 1841 provides the first complete survey of field-names in the parish. This is a valuable historical record and these field-names are reproduced here. For ease of presentation the parish has been split into five (although there is some overlap); a key to the five parts of the parish is provided in Figure 48, and these parts are shown in detail in Figures 49-53. As in Figure 43, dashed lines indicate a line of division between owners where there is no hedge or fence on the ground. Each figure contains a grid to allow individual fields to be located; for example, grid ref A4 is the lower left grid square, C1 the upper right square.

As well as providing an important historical record, the Tithe Map field-names are worth further investigation, since, like place-names, they may contain valuable information about the history of a place. Field-names have been less studied than place-names, but their importance has been recognised for at least 70 years by the English Place-Name Society and other academic bodies, and more attention has been given to their study in recent years. For a recent local study see *Pensford, Publow and Woollard: A Topographical History* by Rowland Janes (2003).

The typical form of field-names differs from that of place-names, as they are usually made up of two words, for example Clover Ground, High Mead or Tee Paddock. In these cases the second word is a generic term for some type of enclosed area, and is likely to occur frequently in a list of names. This second term is usually called the denominative component, while the first word is called the qualifier or specific. Explanations of field names usually focus on the qualifier, although the denominatives can also provide information.

Field-names come in many types besides this simple two-word form. There are single words, some of which may have started life as two words, for example Buryfield and Haymead, while single-word forms, for example Legs and Stews, have a different history. There are cases like Broad Mead Paddock where there are two denominatives, and Little Stable Field which has two qualifiers, and even Great Honey Mead Hill which has two qualifiers and two denominatives.

As well as the many different forms that field-names can take there are other factors which make their study difficult. The tradition is largely verbal, and there are far fewer written records of field-names compared to place-names, with most references dating back only to the 18th and 19th centuries. Field-names are less permanent, and often change completely or more subtly over quite short periods of time, for example by changes in the recorded spelling. Fields themselves change too, and may be amalgamated or divided as farming practices change.

Often there will be several alternative possible explanations of the meaning of a field-name; in such cases the possibilities need to be evaluated in conjunction with what is known about the

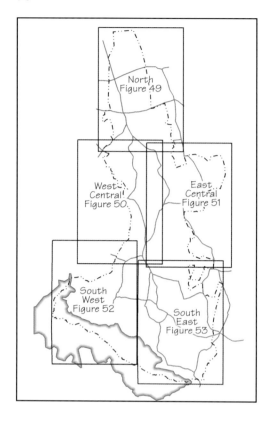

Figure 48: Tithe Map field-names: key to Figures 49-53

site, including such factors as the topography, nearness to water, and the presence of archaeological remains, so as to come to a possible conclusion as to which is the most likely explanation to be correct.

With these "health warnings" of the difficulty of the task and uncertainties involved, an analysis of the meaning of the field names of the Tithe Map is presented in the Appendix, focusing on the qualifier. In some cases earlier field-name evidence is also included. Field-names are arranged there alphabetically by qualifier (or the major qualifier when there are two, so Great Honey Mead Hill is under Honey). If the first word is an obvious qualifier but the second word is not then the first word is ignored, for example Upper Morleys is found under Morleys. Certain straightforward names like Six Acres and Little Field are not discussed and neither are those named after places, for example Bicknell Paddock. The location of the fields in the Appendix is cross-referenced to Figures 49-53.

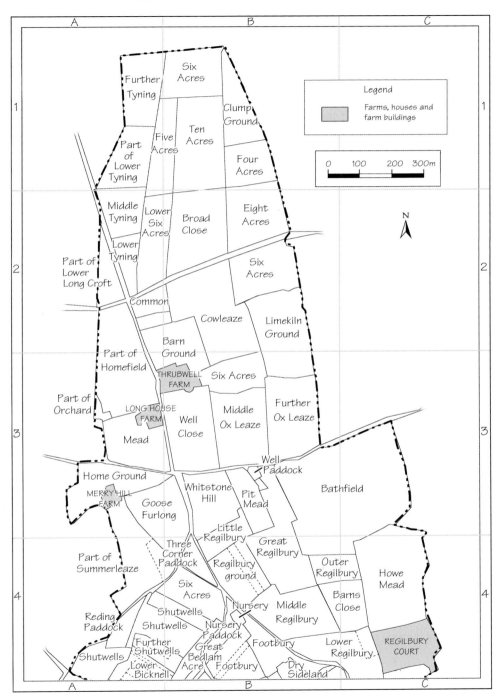

Figure 49: Tithe Map field-names: north

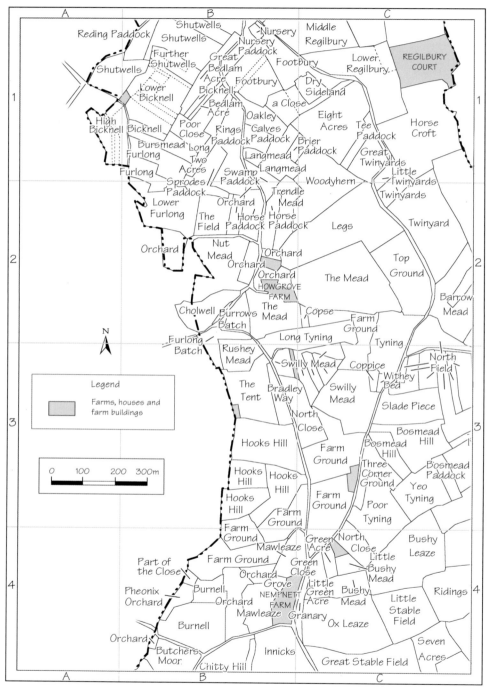

Figure 50: Tithe Map field-names: west central

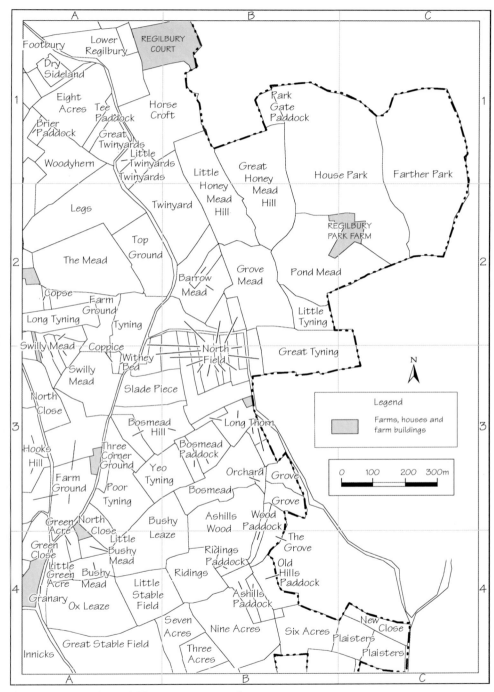

Figure 51: Tithe Map field-names: east central

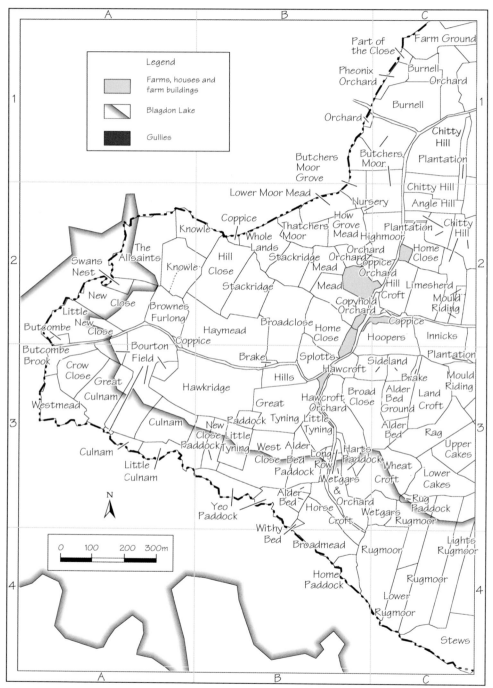

Figure 52: Tithe Map field-names: south west

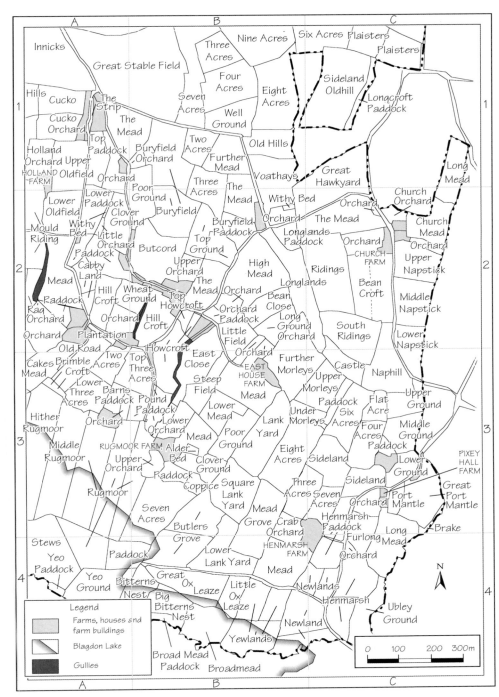

Figure 53: Tithe Map field-names: south-east

The Tithe field-names contain many curiosities. Some field-names seem strange, but have ready explanations: Legs, just to the north-east of Howgrove Farm (Figure 50, grid ref C2), refers to the shape of the field, from an old term for the shape of a stack of corn or hay; Stews, adjacent to the River Yeo and now under Blagdon Lake (Figure 53, A4), comes from a medieval word for fish ponds or tanks; and the Napsticks by the church (Figure 53, C2) probably derive their name from the Old English for a steep hill.

There are fields whose name suggests an interesting and now-lost past; The Allsaints, in the extreme south-west of the parish, now half-submerged by Blagdon Lake (Figure 52, grid ref A2), is indicative of a religious dedication; the names Bedlam Acre and Great Bedlam Acre, north along the lane from Howgrove Farm (Figure 50, B1), usually refer to a place previously connected in some way with the mentally unwell, but no such place is known in Nempnett; and the name Plaisters, which occurs twice just north of the church and near what we now call Plaster's Green (Figure 53, C1, is usually taken to indicate an old meeting place.

As well as the many individual examples of unusual names a more general analysis of field-names can also be informative. Those fields whose names or shapes are suggestive of open-fields or woodland clearance are shown Figure 54. The first category includes names such as Furlong, Innicks and Shutwells, all terms associated with open-field systems, and distinctively shaped fields (as discussed earlier in this chapter). The latter category includes fields with the denominatives croft, riding or wood, for example Hill Croft, The Ridings and Ashills, as these names are often associated with medieval enclosure of woodland, and names such as Morleys where the -ley suggests a woodland clearing.

Comparing Figure 54 with Figure 43 we would expect the "open-field names/shapes" to fall into area 4, and the "clearing names" into area 5. Generally this is the case, suggesting that the county-wide classification of Figure 43 is fairly accurate in the parish, although there are one or two exceptions, which suggests the classification may require some "fine tuning".

Field-names which usually are taken to indicate the presence in the field, or nearby, of some noteworthy archaeological feature are shown in Figure 55, along with the archaeological sites, both definite and speculative, discussed in Chapter 2. Many "archaeological" field-names are near known sites: the Bourton Fields are close to the Hawkridge Barrow, the Burnells close to

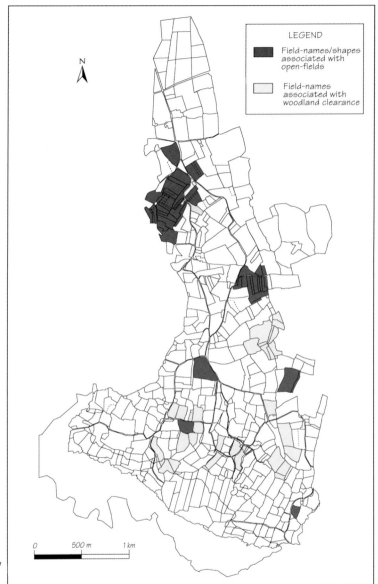

Figure 54: Field-names of the Tithe Map suggestive of open-fields and woodland clearance

the oval enclosure SMR 5300, Bursmead is near the Bicknell Barrow, and the Footburys are close to Regilbury.

However, some "archaeological" field-names have no known feature nearby, and may therefore be indicative of undiscovered archaeology in the parish. For example, the two field-names

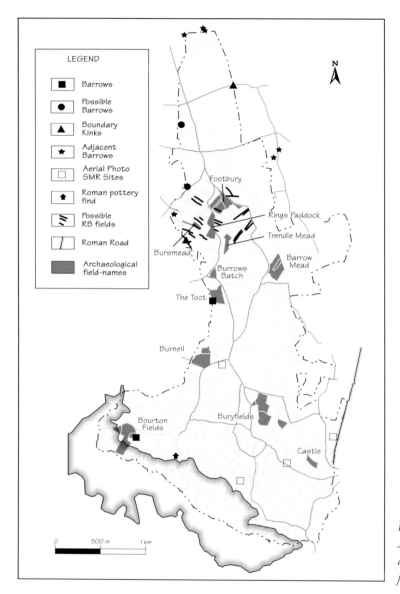

Figure 55:
Archaeological sites
and "archaeological"
field-names

Rings Paddock and Trendle Mead, just north of Howgrove
Farm and close to each other and in an area known to have been
settled at least as long ago as the Iron Age, may be referring to an
unknown prehistoric circular enclosure. Second, there is a cluster
of Buryfield names on the high plateau land in the centre of the
parish, with the field Castle just to the south-east, names usually
of archaeological significance. There are no known archaeological

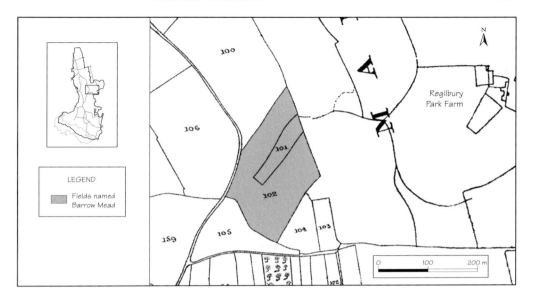

Figure 56: Extract from the 1841 Tithe Map showing the Barrow Mead fields

features in this area, but the presence of these field-names plus the proximity of the Roman road and two SMR sites suggests this area might deserve investigation.

A third example are the two fields named Barrow Mead, just to the south-west of Regilbury. This is a highly suggestive name, and an extract from the Tithe Map for this area is shown in Figure 56. At the time of the Tithe Map there were two fields named Barrow Mead, numbered 101 and 102, the smaller measuring *c.* 100 m by 20m and looking of suitable shape to have at one time enclosed a barrow. By the time of the first Ordnance Survey map in 1888 these two fields had merged, and today there is no obvious sign of a prehistoric feature, but the area might be worth further study.

CONCLUSIONS

This chapter has drawn together material on the fields and field-names of the parish, largely based on the evidence provided by the Tithe Map. The pattern of fields throughout the parish suggests settlement developed first in the northern "plateau" of the parish, and later extended to the more southerly, steeply sloping land. Probably most of the parish was settled by the medieval period, and there has been remarkably little change since then. Much of the landscape of the parish today probably dates back 700 years, but in places there may still be remnants of pre-historic and/or Roman fields dating back thousands of years.

The field-names of the Tithe Map are an intriguing insight into the past; all the names must once have been readily understood, but over time the meaning has become more difficult to understand, perhaps because the features to which they once referred have now disappeared, or because of changes to the language we use. The field-names discussed here are a valuable record of the history of the parish, and an invitation to the curious to try and resolve the remaining uncertainties about their meaning.

6   Regilbury Manor 1086-1536

INTRODUCTION

Manors were central to the economic and social life of the English countryside from Saxon times right through to the late 19th century. Over much of this period manors provided justice, controlled land ownership, and could be instrumental in radical changes to rural areas, for example by the development of country parks or new villages. Thus, manorial records provide an important insight into the medieval period, and for the first time in the history of the parish we can identify individuals who lived in Nempnett Thrubwell and played a role in village life those many centuries ago.

For the medieval and later periods documents are the main source of information, particularly for Nempnett where there has been little in the way of archaeological excavations. However, few records survive, and the information they provide is selective, with even the Domesday Book, that key reference for English local history, providing information that is at times the subject of much discussion and uncertainty. Also, it is often much easier to discover the line of ownership of a manor than to determine exactly where it was and what area its lands covered, so that tracing which manor or manors are relevant to a particular parish is not a straightforward task.

The current state of knowledge suggests that the manorial history of Nempnett Thrubwell is particularly complex. In his pioneering work on the geography of Somerset as recorded in the Domesday Book, published in 1880, the Rev Eyton writes: "Manorially, we suggest, the whole parish [of Nempnett

Thrubwell] consisted of parcels taken from diverse Domesday manors".[1] Ninety years later Francis Neale reaches a similar conclusion, as her work on Butcombe describes "a confusing and occasionally conflicting series of genealogies and property transfers" involving manors owning land in Butcombe, Nempnett, and other nearby parishes.[2]

This chapter is the first of four which address the manorial history of Nempnett Thrubwell. Here the focus is the Manor of Regilbury, mainly its ownership, over the period 1086-1536; chapter 7 discusses the period 1537-1860; chapter 8 addresses in more detail what is known about the geography of the Manor of Regilbury in 1730; and chapter 9 discusses a number of other manors that are thought to have had connections with the parish.

THE MANOR OF REGILBURY 1086-1860: AN OVERVIEW

Figure 57 presents an overview of the "timeline" of Regilbury Manor, which shows the known owners over the period 1086-1860. At the time of the Domesday Book in 1086 Serlo de Burci, a Norman baron and major landowner in the South West of England, owned the Manor, then known as Ragiol. From him it passed to his direct descendants the Martins. At some time in the 12th or 13th century, possibly 1193, the manor passed into the hands of Flaxley Abbey, a small Cistercian Monastery in the Forest of Dean.

At the dissolution of the monasteries in 1536-7 Regilbury came into the possession of Sir William Kingston, a favourite of Henry VIII, and his family held it until 1565, when it passed briefly through the hands of Edward Barnard to reach the Babers in 1566. The Baber family were major landowners in the Chew Valley, the Wrington Vale, and elsewhere in north Somerset at that time. In 1715 the property passed from the Babers to the Tyntes of Goathurst near Bridgwater, later known as the Kemeys-Tyntes, who retained interests in Regilbury and Nempnett into the 20th century.

Although Figure 57 and this brief description provide a neat and tidy picture of the Manor over 850 years, there are still many uncertainties and unknowns. In particular it is only in the 18th century that we are able to get a clear picture of exactly what lands were owned by the manor. The degree to which the extent

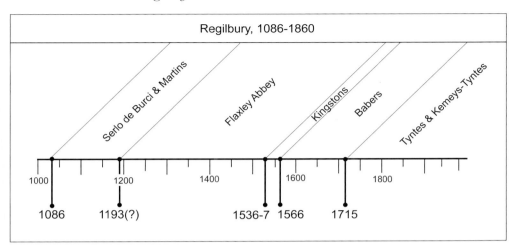

Figure 57: Regilbury Manor summary timeline 1066-1860

of lands owned by the manor changed over time is very difficult to determine. Some of the uncertainties and difficulties in the interpretation of the history of Regilbury Manor are covered in the next few sections, where the first part of this timeline is discussed in more detail.

THE DOMESDAY BOOK: OVERVIEW

In 1066, probably the best-known date in English history, William of Normandy conquered England, and soon after most of the lands of the English nobility were granted to his followers. Twenty years later the Domesday Book was compiled to determine what exactly was held by each landowner, and this source is one of the most important documents in any study of local history.

The Domesday Book set out to record the details of land ownership across the country so that "every man should know his right and not usurp another's." The country was divided into counties, and then further into hundreds, and commissioners were sent to each hundred to collect evidence on oath from knowledgeable individuals.

Information was collected by hundred, but was then re-arranged to be published collated by landowner. In Somerset, however, there are two versions of this "final" Domesday Book, which are called the Exeter and the Exchequer. There are many differences between the two, and experts are unable to agree on which is the more accurate. Many of the discrepancies appear to have arisen through omissions and careless copying. A further complication is that there are two lists of hundreds bound up with the Exeter version that do not agree with each other, so that even the allocation of manors to hundreds is not straightforward. There are today manors referred to as "lost", that is to say whose geographical location is not known, and others whose exact location and extent is still the subject of debate.

Despite these complications the Domesday Book is a key source for all local historians. The commissioners asked for information about each estate or land holding, and used a specific set of questions, namely:

> The name of the place. Who held it, before 1066, and now?
> How many hides? How many ploughs, both those in lordship and the men's?
> How many villagers, cottagers and slaves, how many free men and Freemen?
> How much woodland, meadow and pasture? How many mills and fishponds?
> How much has been added or taken away? What the total value was and is?
> How much each free man or Freeman had or has? All threefold, before 1066, when King William gave it, and now; and if more can be had than at present?

Some of these questions require clarification. The hide is a measure of land, the exact meaning of which is still debated. It is often translated as a fixed unit of area, usually said to equal 120 acres, but it seems more likely that it was a unit of taxation assessment, a further sub-division of the hundred, so that a direct correlation to area is not possible. Where subdivision was necessary virgates were used, with four virgates to a hide. A plough was a plough-team, usually of eight oxen, used to cultivate the arable land, and probably a typical plough-team would work 120 acres. Many of the detailed returns for the area under woodland, meadow, and pasture appear to be too imprecise for detailed analysis.

The Domesday Book recorded six types of individual, or social group, as follows:

villagers or **villeins** were unfree tenants who held their land subject to a range of agricultural services and fines. Neither a villager nor his daughter could marry without the Lord's permission, nor could he bring suit in the court, or acquire land that would not be taxed. Upon his death a tax called a heriot, often the best beast on the farm, was paid by his heirs. In return the villein had a land holding and the right to graze a fixed number of cattle on the common pastures and to take hay from the common meadow,

bordars or **smallholders** had some land for subsistence but were obliged to perform agricultural and menial services for the Lord free, or for a fixed fee,

slaves or **serfs** were landless bondmen tied to the Lord's person and who could be sold to another person,

cottagers or **cottars** were not tied to the land but were expected to work for the Lord one day a week,

coliberts, 'distinctly superior to the serfs but distinctly inferior to the villains, bordars and cottars', were found mainly on Royal estates in Somerset, and

miscellaneous, including swineherds, fishermen, smiths and priests.

Land on an estate was divided into two types, that held directly by the Lord, which is called "in demesne" or in lordship, and that held by villagers, bordars, cottars and coliberts.

THE DOMESDAY BOOK: RAGIOL

There are two entries in the Domesday Book for the Manor of Regilbury, then spelt Ragiol. The first is under the heading "Land of Serlo de Burci" and reads thus:

> Guntard holds Ragiol from Serlo. Four thanes held it before 1066; it paid tax for 2 hides. Land for 2 ploughs. In lordship 1 plough with 1 slave and 1 villager. Meadow, 5 acres; underwood, 5 acres. 15 cattle; 6 pigs; 55 sheep. Value 30s [£1.50]; when Serlo acquired it 20s [£1].

> 1 hide and 1 virgate of land have been added to this [manor]. A thane held them freely before 1066. Land for 3 ploughs. Walter holds [it] from Serlo; he [Walter] has

1 plough there, in lordship; 4 slaves with 1 villager and 1 smallholder. Meadow 3 acres; woodland, 3 furlongs in length and as much in width. 1 riding-horse; 4 cattle; 10 pigs. [Value] formerly 10s [50p]; now 30s [£1.50]. This land did not belong to Everwacer.

The entry is for two estates. The first estate is of 2 hides and is held by Guntard, who would have been a sub-tenant of Serlo. A 2-hide estate is fairly small. For example Ubley and Norton Malreward were 5 hide estates, Winford, Barrow Gurney, Backwell, Blagdon, Clutton, Compton Martin, West Harptree, East Harptree and (probably) Chew Stoke were 10 hide estates, and Wrington and Chew Magna were 20 hides. The nearest in size were Butcombe (3 hides) and Aldwick (2 hides). Using these neighbouring parishes to give a very rough estimate suggests a hide equates to about 250 acres, so this estate might have been of the order of roughly 500 acres.

Guntard (also spelt Gontar) held only this one manor in Somerset. Guntard held about half the land (one plough out of two) in his demesne, the remainder being worked by a villager. The estate is notable for the large number of sheep, which suggests it may have included high land on Broadfield Down.

The second estate that was added to the first, and is sometimes called an *additamentum*, is of 1¼ hides (one hide and one virgate), perhaps 300 acres. The sub-tenant in charge of this estate is written in various ways in different versions and translations, with a first name of either Walter or William and a surname of Hussey, Hosed or Hosate. It seems likely that this is the Hosate family who are known to have held land in Nempnett in the 12th and 13th centuries. William Hosate also held two other manors in Somerset as a sub-tenant (Stratton-on-Fosse and Charlecombe), while a Walter Hosate held three manors as a sub-tenant (Bath Easton, Priston and Whatley nr Frome). William Hosate is also noted to have purchased the 50 hide Manor of Keynsham for £80 and to have held the Manor of Tadwick directly from the King as a "Franci Tegni" or French Thane.

It seems from this that the Hosate family must have been fairly important. The presence of four slaves and a riding-horse on the estate may be another indication of a higher than average status for a small estate. Roughly a third of the land was in demesne, with the remainder of the land in the control of a villager and a cottar. That this estate had three ploughs, whereas the first estate had two, perhaps suggests a lower elevation with more arable land.

The significance of the final sentence "this land did not belong to Everwacer", which appears to refer to both estates, is that whereas Serlo de Burci's ordinary title was as successor to the estates of the Saxon Everwacer (also spelt Alwacre, Euroacre, Euerwacher, and Euroacro), he derived these estates from no such antecessor. In the Exeter version of the Domesday Book these two estates are described as being an *additamentum* to Serlo de Burci's estate at Aldwick, suggesting an early link between Regilbury and Aldwick Manors.

A second entry for Ragiol is under the heading "What the King's Clergy (hold)" or "Land which has been given to the saints in almoin" and reads as follows:

> Godwin holds ½ hide in the manor called Ragiol in alms from the King. He had the whole manor before, in 1066. Value 3s [15p].

Godwin is also known as "Godwin the Englishman." The relationship between this estate and the other two at Ragiol is not clear; Godwin might have been one of the unnamed Thanes who before 1066 held one of Serlo de Burci's estates at Regilbury. A half-hide estate might have been of the order of 125 acres. That such an entry exists suggests very strongly that there was a church in Nempnett or Regilbury at the time of the conquest.

SERLO DE BURCI AND THE MARTIN FAMILY

Serlo de Burci is thought to have derived his surname from a place near Vire in the Calvados department in France and was a major landholder in England at the time of the Domesday Book. He was tenant-in-chief of lands at Blagdon, Uphill, Chew Stoke, Chillyhill (also Chew Stoke), Aldwick, Ragiol, Kilmington, Lovington, Wheathill, Compton Martin, Morton, Mudford, and Stone in Somerset. In Dorset, he was tenant-in-chief of lands at Puddle and Whitcliff. He furthermore held land under the King at Kilmington and Congresbury, under the Bishop of Bath at Banwell, and under the Abbey of Glastonbury at Low Ham, Pylle, Monkton, and Hornblotton, in Somerset, and at Tidpit in Damerham, Wiltshire. He also held many lordships in Cheshire.

It is thought that his principal residence in Somerset was at Blagdon.

Figure 58 shows that part of the family tree of Serlo de Burci as affects Regilbury and Nempnett. He appears to have died around 1086 and to have left two daughters by a wife whose name is not known. One of these daughters, whose name is also unknown, became a nun at Shaftsbury, and thus relinquished all claims on Serlo's property. Serlo's daughter Geva thus inherited all of Serlo's estate. She married twice, firstly to one Martin and then to William de Falaise. Regilbury passed to the Martin branch of the family, along with the majority of Serlo's holdings.

Very little is known of Geva's first husband Martin, other than that he died before 1086 and left a son called Robert who was known as Robert fitz Martin (Robert son of Martin). In the 12th century there are many records of this Robert, notably in connection with his donations to many existing religious houses and the establishment of the abbey at St. Dogmaels, Dyfed, in 1155. Such donations of land were very common in the 12th and 13th century, to such a degree that it is claimed that by 1278 over 70% of the land in England was under Church control. Watkins explains it thus:

> "Rich estate owners and others, fearful of their destination on death, frequently gave land to the Church, or founded Chantries, where priests were paid to pray daily for the soul of the donor in the devout belief that this would ensure undisturbed repose in Paradise until the resurrection morning, when soul and body would meet again to enjoy everlasting life".[3]

An important charter of Henry II, thought to date to 1155, gives the King's reaffirmation of Robert fitz Martin's right to the lands of his grandfather Serlo de Burci. The charter reads:

> Henry, King of the English, Duke of the Normans and of the people of Aquitaine and Count of the people of Anjou to all Archbishops, Bishops, Counts, Barons, Viscounts and all kinsmen and faithful subjects of England and Normandy, greetings.
>
> Know that I have surrendered and granted to Robert Fitz Martin all the land of Serlo de Burci, his grandfather, thus freely, with immunity and honourably to be held as

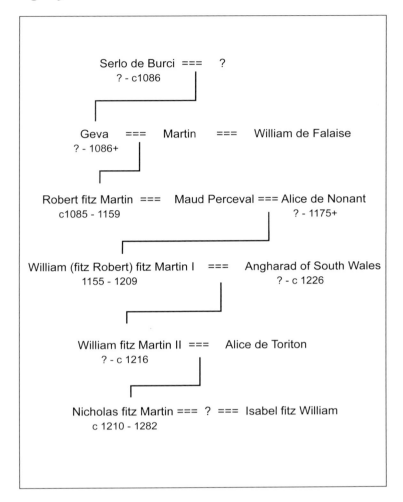

Figure 58: Serlo de Burci and Martins family tree

ever Serlo himself held the land or any of his predecessors held that land in the time of my predecessors, better and more freely and more quietly and more honourably, with all the freedoms and dues in woods and level country, in meadows and pasture land, in waters and elsewhere, with the right of manorial jurisdiction and infangenoteof. These rights I concede to him in covenant and heredity to be held by him and his heirs from me and my heirs, in lands and warrens and in all other matters.

Witnessed by: The Lord Chancellor, Roger Count of Hereford, Hunfridus de Bohun, Chamberlain Warinus Fitz Gerold, Hubert de Vallibus, Henry Hosate, Hugo Hosate, Willeimus Malet, at Walengeford.[4]

Some of the terms used here deserve clarification. Manorial jurisdiction was the privilege enjoyed by the Lord of the Manor of holding courts, trying causes and imposing fines, and infangenoteof was the right, granted by the king, to hang a thief caught "hand-having or back bearing", that is to say "red-handed", with stolen goods upon ones own land. It is also notable that among the witnesses to this charter are Henry and Hugo Hosate, an indication that the Hosate family must have been of some substance to be present at this gathering.

Robert fitz Martin lived from about 1085 to 1159, and married twice, to Maud Perceval and Alice de Nonant. Robert's heir, by his second wife, was William fitz Martin I (1155-1209), sometimes known as William fitz Robert fitz Martin. This William married Angharad, or Ankaret, a daughter of Rhys ap Gruffyd, from South Wales, and his heir was William fitz Martin II, followed by Sir Nicholas Martin. It appears that the Martin family held a large barony centred on Blagdon, and which included lands in Aldwick and Nempnett Thrubwell, continuously through to 1325. At some stage in this period, however, control of the Manor of Regilbury passed to Flaxley Abbey.

A final point on the de Burci family is that two individuals of this name appear in the Cartulary of Flaxley Abbey. Philip de Burci is mentioned in the context of a grant of the estate of Regilbury, and Galfrido de Burci is a witness to grants of land from Regilbury; both references are thought to date to c. 1200.[5] The usual lineage of Serlo de Burci, as shown in Figure 58, has no male offspring, so the relationship between Serlo, and Galfrido and Philip is unknown.

FLAXLEY ABBEY

The Cistercian Abbey of Flaxley, sometimes called Dene Abbey or the Abbey of the Blessed Mary of Dean, was founded by Roger Fitzwalter, Earl of Hereford, between 1151 and 1154, at a site some 15km south-west of Gloucester in the Forest of Dean – see Figure 59. Legend has it that the site of the abbey

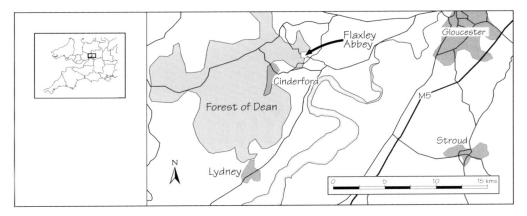

Figure 59: Flaxley Abbey location map

marks the exact spot of the death of Roger's father Milo, who was murdered on Christmas Eve 1143 whilst out hunting deer in the Forest.

At this time the Cistercian Order of Monks was held in high regard. The Cistercians taught and practised the virtue of hard work, and they had a reputation for bringing peace, prosperity and employment to the land they settled. To be a suitable site for a monastery a potential site had to be

> "in a remote and solitary place, fit for habitation, fertile, good for fruit, suitable for grain, buried in woods, alongside a river or stream, abounding in springs, a place apart from the haunts of men where the Monks could live in silence and austerity".[6]

In one respect though Flaxley was unusual. For some time the Forest of Dean had been used by the King and his court for the sport of hunting deer, and Earl Roger wished this to continue using Flaxley as the base. He decided, with the approval of the Order, to include a large Guest Hall in the Monastery for such visits where the future King could entertain his guests in some splendour and comfort, hoping that the Abbey would receive favours from the King in return. As a result the Abbey included "The Kings Hall", a self-contained unit which could seat 200 and which had adjacent a bakehouse, brew-house, kitchen and stores and ample dormitories set somewhat aside from the other areas of the Abbey.

For two centuries after its instigation Flaxley was closely linked to the Crown, and received many favours from successive Kings, notably in the granting of lands and favourable court rulings. In return Flaxley occasionally housed the King and his court at great hunting and religious feasts. However, the income of Flaxley was never particularly large and in the 13th and 14th centuries the Abbey was frequently in debt. Edward III was the last royal patron, and after his death in 1377 the monks continued their Cistercian way of life removed from the Court's affairs.

It is known that at the time of dissolution (1536-7) Flaxley Abbey owned Regilbury Manor, then spelt Rochelbury or Rothelbury. Exactly how the Manor came into the hands of Flaxley, and the differences, if any, between the extent and nature of "Regilbury Manor" in 1086 and 1536 are questions we are unlikely to be able to answer with any certainty. However, it is clear that in the second half of the 12th century there were many links between Flaxley, Nempnett and Regilbury.

There is a local belief that King John visited Regilbury Manor sometime around 1207-9 although the basis for this is unclear, but the royal link with Flaxley gives some credence to this tale.

THE CARTULARY OF FLAXLEY ABBEY *c.* 1200

Our knowledge of these early days of Flaxley Abbey is largely due to the survival of "The Cartulary of Flaxley Abbey," a manuscript which records all the major transactions of the Abbey up to about 1200, and which is now preserved in the British Museum. The Cartulary is:

> "a very long roll of vellum, which was the form used before books came into general use, approximately 11in [30cm] wide, extending to some 20ft [6m], which was beautifully written in the 12th Century, and gives a most interesting and valuable record of the chief items of the Abbey's transactions during this period".[7]

Somehow this document was smuggled away from the attentions of the Commissioners of Henry VIII, and it then lay undiscovered for nearly 300 years until it was found among the possessions of Thomas Wynniatt Esq. of Stanton in Gloucestershire. It was then translated by Sir Thomas Phillips

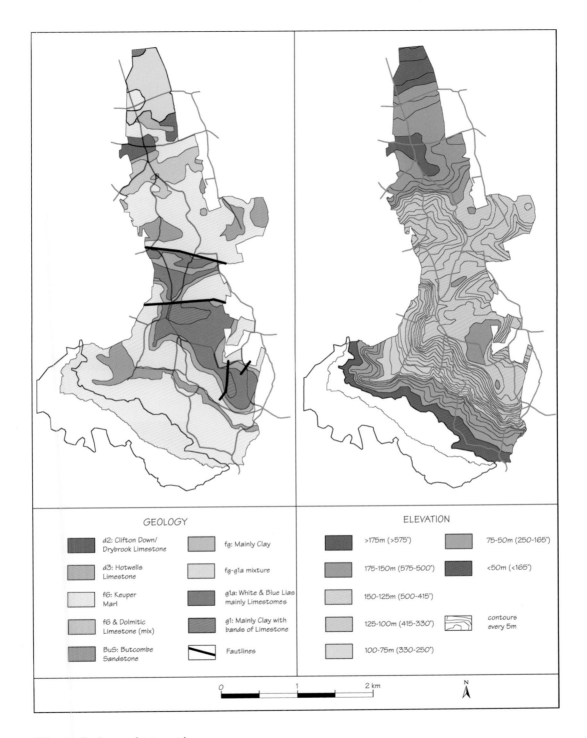

GEOLOGY

- d2: Clifton Down/ Drybrook Limestone
- d3: Hotwells Limestone
- f6: Keuper Marl
- f6 & Dolmitic Limestone (mix)
- BuS: Butcombe Sandstone
- fg: Mainly Clay
- fg-g1a mixture
- g1a: White & Blue Lias mainly Limestomes
- g1: Mainly Clay with bands of Limestone
- Fautlines

ELEVATION

- >175m (>575')
- 175-150m (575-500')
- 150-125m (500-415')
- 125-100m (415-330')
- 100-75m (330-250')
- 75-50m (250-165')
- <50m (<165')
- contours every 5m

0   1   2 km

N

Plate 1: Geology and topography

Plate 2: St. Mary's church: setting

Plate 3: St. Mary's church: building and yard

Plate 4: Nempnett Street

Plate 5: West Town

Plate 6: Hawkridge, Chitty Hill and Blagdon Lake

Plate 7: Butcombe Court Barrow

Plate 8: Bicknell and Bicknell Farm

Plate 9: The site of Fairy's Toot

Plate 10: Stoney Littleton: entrance

Plate 11: Stoney Littleton: internal chamber

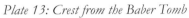

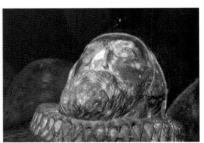

Plate 13: Crest from the Baber Tomb

Plate 14: Detail from the Baber Tomb

Plate 12: The Baber Tomb, St. Andrew's church Chew Magna

Plate 15: Detail from the
Baber Tomb

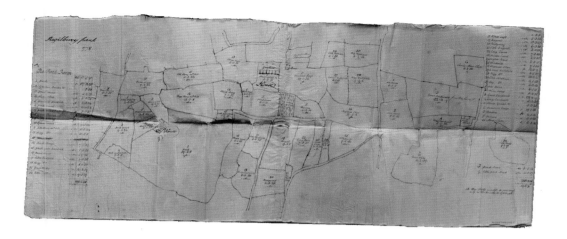

Plate 16: Plan of Regilbury Court, Park Farm and Crudwells Tenement, 1778

*Plate 17: Regilbury
Court Farm from the
south-east*

*Plate 18: Regilbury
Court Farm from the
north-east*

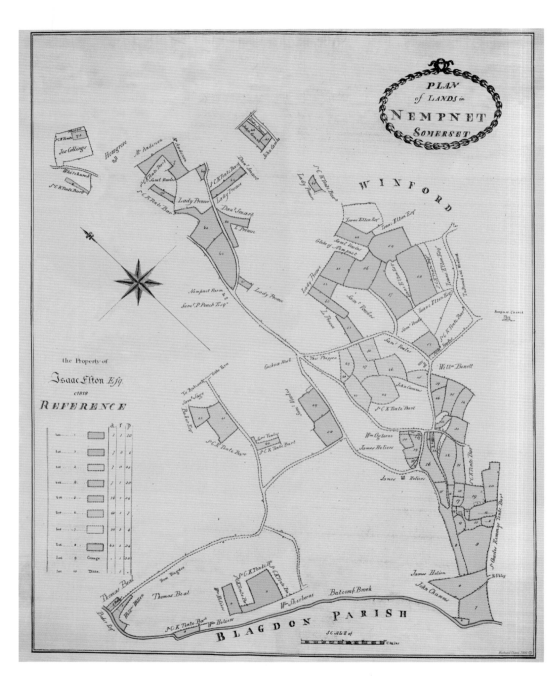

Plate 19: Map of Isaac Elton's lands in Nempnett, c. 1818

and later published by A W Crawley-Boevey in 1887 under the title *The Cartulary and Historical Notes of the Cistercian Abbey of Flaxley Abbey*. The Cartulary provides information on the rents payable to and by the Abbey, the rent granted in alms to provide for the sick and poor, and the grants of land made to the Abbey, as well as further information about the running of the Abbey and the contents of its library. There are many mentions of Nempnett, Regilbury and Thrubwell in the Cartulary, and these are now discussed, starting with grants of land.

In 1193 a grant of "the whole estate of Ragel with appurtenances" was made to the Abbey. The chain of ownership is complicated. Philip de Burci first gave the land to William de Sancto Leodegario (William of St. Leger) in perpetuity for an annual rent of two shillings [10p]. In return William de Sancto Leodegario settled a debt of 87½ marks [about £58] that Philip de Burci owed to Manasser, a Jew of Bristol. William de Sancto Leodegario then granted the land to Flaxley to be held at ⅔ of a knight's fee, and for a yearly rent of two shillings [10p], which after 30 years had elapsed was to be paid, with an additional two shillings, to Phillip de Burci and his heirs. William and his heirs received at the same time the perpetual right of presenting one monk to the Abbey and he and his heirs were received both in life and death into all the benefits of the church.[8]

These grants were given formal confirmation by "William fitz Robert fitz Martin, wife of Ankaret", who is described as the superior lord. This mention of William fitz Robert fitz Martin, who was Serlo be Burci's great-grandson (see Figure 58), seems to confirm that this was part of Domesday Ragiol, probably the estate in the sub-tenancy of Guntard.

The reference to ⅔ of a knight's fee is worth further comment. When the Normans conquered England they introduced feudal law, based upon a military plan. The kingdom was divided into what were called "knights' fees", of which there were about 60,000, and for every knight's fee a knight or soldier was obliged to attend the king in his wars for a certain period each year. Lists of these knights' fees exist for various dates from the 12th to 15th century and can provide valuable information in tracking the ownership of estates. That the land transferred to Flaxley warranted ⅔ of a knight's fee suggests a considerable estate.

There are three grants of land by Walter and Robert Sprot of Ragel. The first is "a certain croft in Ragelbury [also spelt Rachelbury], near St. Andrew's fountain, and between the garden which used to belong to Philip de Burci and the house of Oswald." The second is of "two acres of land towards the south, lying between two acres of Emnet [Nempnett], and the croft which belonged to Ailward le Siegneur, and half an acre of meadow lying adjacent to the aforesaid two acres in Duddemead." The third, from Walter Sprot, is "of the whole of his portion of certain land in the hills, reckoned about four and a half acres: also common of pasture, both in the hills and the fields".[9]

Hugh Hosate, who in one document is described as "Hugo Hosate of Emptione [Nempnett]" also gave land to the Abbey. One grant speaks of "two acres of land in Ragelbury, lying near the road towards the south, between the house of Ailward le Siegneur, and the house of Galfrid Tripel," for which the monks of Flaxley apparently paid the sum of six shillings [30p]. In the royal charter of 1227 in which Henry III confirmed various grants to Flaxley there is reference to "the gift of Hugh Hosate of all his land at Emmett [Nempnett] with appurtenances".[10]

Another reference that gives further details of the relationship between Hugh Hosate and Flaxley is to be found in the Curia Regis Rolls (the proceedings of the King's Court) for 1208. The full entry (translated from the Latin, but still very legalistic in its language) is:

> Hugo Hose, when summoned to show why he was not keeping the agreement between himself and Abbot de Flexel' concerning four virgates with appurtenances in Emnet, concerning which a signed document was produced between them in the King's Court concerning the warranty of the deed in which the signed deed is contained which Hugo warranted to the aforesaid abbot and his successors to hold concerning himself and his heirs through villein tenure of one mark of cash during the year for service at the feast of St. Michael, excepting only the King's service, comes and speaks because his master demands from him help for the knighting of his son and the marriage of his daughter and feudal due on the aforesaid land; and therefore it seems to him that this same abbot owes to him concerning the land; and the abbot seeks the judgment of the Court whether he must give that service just as the signed deed testifies that he owes nothing except the one marc annually royal service. From which it has been judged that the same Hugo or his heirs will not be able to

enforce the aforesaid services because it is not service to the king.[11]

Translated from the legal terms this reference tells the following story. At some time Hugo Hose conveyed or gave to the Abbot of Flaxley his land in Nempnett. The terms of the agreement were that the Abbot would pay Hugo one silver mark [13s 4d, or 67p] per year at Michaelmas in return for which Hugo would meet any legal burdens due on the land, except demands from the King which the Abbot would have to meet. The Abbey was then free to make as much profit from the land as it could. Now Hugo's overlord, who is unnamed, has demanded from Hugo further payments, as was his feudal right, to help the Lord pay for the cost of knighting his son and marrying his daughter (that is to say the Lord's son and daughter). Hugo has passed on these demands to the Abbot, but the Abbot has refused to pay saying Hugo should meet these burdens. The court agreed with the Abbot, saying that these extra taxes would have to be met by Hugo, since the original agreement said Hugo would have to meet all taxes raised on the land except those raised by the King, and these demands were not from the King.

The reference describes the land in question as "four virgates with appurtenances in Nempnett." Although such estimates of the amount of land tend to be somewhat notional, a four virgate, or one hide, estate is quite substantial. It seems likely, given the sub-tenant's name and the size of the estate, that this land is some, or possibly all, of the five virgate estate of Ragiol sub-tenanted to William Hosate in the Domesday Book. If that is indeed the case it seems that all of the land within the Ragiol Domesday manor may have passed to Flaxley Abbey by the early 13th century.

Within the Cartulary there is also a brief mention of a gift of Peter de Salso Mariso (Peter of Salt Marsh) of "all his land in Tribnell [Tribnelle] with all appurtenances," which is generally regarded as an early reference to Thrubwell.

The Cartulary also records that the Abbey paid a yearly rent to the church at Emnet [Nempnett] of one shilling and two pence [6p], and a yearly rent of two shillings [10p] to the church at Budichumbe [Butcombe]. The payment to Butcombe Church is documented as being due to an agreement made between Walter of Butcombe and Flaxley that the tithes due on seven acres of Walter's land be given to the monks, in exchange for which the Abbey gave two shillings [10p] to the Church. Presumably a similar agreement must have been reached involving Nempnett Church although no record survives.

On the deeds and grants recorded in the Cartulary there are usually named witnesses, and these are of interest as they show the persons of chief local importance at the time. Some names appear over and over again suggesting that the owners must have been on very intimate terms with the Flaxley monks. Amongst these frequent witnesses is Godfrey Chaplain of Emnet (recorded as Godefrido Capellano de Emnet and Godfrido Sacerdote de Emnet). Given that the date of the Cartulary is late 12th century, it seems likely that Godfrey is the earliest known Chaplain of St. Mary's Church Nempnett.

Amongst the list of private benefactors enumerated in the Flaxley Cartulary are Walter and Robert [Sprot] of Ragel in the County of Somerset, and Hugh Hosate. This is another indication that the Hosates were of some standing.

The Cartulary of Flaxley is important for many reasons. The references to Nempnett, Thrubwell and Regilbury, in their various spellings, are amongst the earliest written records of these names. Their use suggests that these three place-names had separate geographical identities that were of sufficient importance to be included in legal documents. The close links that existed between Regilbury, Nempnett and Flaxley by 1200 are evident. For the first time we have records for individuals; for example it seems likely that Hugh Hosate was an important individual who lived in Nempnett and we know of Godfrey the Chaplain. Walter and Robert Sprot appear to be been important in Regilbury.

OTHER EARLY SOURCES

There are very few other sources of information for the period 1200-1536. What little data are available come from two main sources, lists of knights' fees, which were made periodically to assist the State's finances, and the occasional surviving deed, usually to do with land transfers.

In the early 14th century there are a series of references to the de Rilleburys' at Regilbury. Peter de Rillebury of Raggel appears in the Nomina Villarium of 1316, a return not strictly concerned with Military Tenures but usually treated in a similar way to the knights' fees.[12] And Robert and Peter de Rillebury appear as witnesses to a deed between Johanna Perceval-Bretasche and the Hospital of St. John the Baptist dated 1314 and signed at Thrubwell.[13]

From 1284 to 1428 there are a series of entries for Sprotragel, in various spellings, which are usually attributed to Regilbury. In 1284 in survey known as Kirkby's Quest there is the entry "Johannes Sparke holds a quarter of a knight's fee at Sprocrashele of Herberto de Sancto Quintino." Exactly the same entry is to be found in the return of 1303. An entry for 1346 reads "Jososa de Bayouse holds a quarter of a knight's fee in Sprottragel which Johannes Sparke held before." In 1428 there is an entry that says, "Johanne Rodeney holds ¾ of a knight's fee at Sprottegate which Joceus de Bayus held before".[14]

These four entries thus appear to make a consistent history for the place Sprotragel. This name may derive from a combination of Sprot and Ragel, the Sprot family being prominent at Regilbury around 1200 (see above) and Ragel was the usual spelling at that time. Exactly how this place relates to Regilbury and Flaxley is not clear.

In 1428 there is mention of a new ½ a knight's fee at Troblevill of the Abbot of Flaxley. This may be Thrubwell but the entry is in the Hundred of Keynsham, whereas all the entries for Ragel and Sprotragel are in the Hundred of Portbury, Harecliffe and Bedminster. Related to this there is a previous entry in 1316 in the Hundred of Keynsham for "Staunton Drewe cum hameleto Trubwell" with the names Drogo de Staunton and Johannes Botiller. If these entries are for the Thrubwell of Nempnett parish is not clear how and why the link with Stanton Drew was established.

THE DISSOLUTION OF FLAXLEY

The end of the link between Flaxley Abbey and Regilbury came with the dissolution of the monasteries by Henry VIII in 1536. At the surrender to the king on 4 February 1536 Flaxley's revenues were below £200 a year and there were in residence seven priests, one lay brother and 18 servants. The Abbey has been rebuilt and added to over the years, and parts are still standing today. It is still in use as a private residence, and for generations was in the hands of the Boevey family, later the Crawley-Boeveys. Its more recent history is traced in *Notes on the History of Flaxley Abbey* by Sir Francis Crawley-Boevey published in 1914.

CONCLUSIONS

From 1086 on documentary sources play an increasingly important part in tracing the local history of the parish. This chapter has summarised what is known about Regilbury Manor and its relationship to Nempnett Thrubwell over the period 1086-1536. It is clear that there were important links between Nempnett and Regilbury and therefore between Flaxley Abbey and Nempnett, and the fortuitous survival of the Cartulary of Flaxley means there are some very early records of the parish.

It seems likely from what is recorded in the Domesday Book that there was a church in the parish by 1086, and the Cartulary of Flaxley suggests that Godfrey was chaplain there at around 1200, a fact apparently not previously known as his name does not appear in the church list of rectors. The records of Flaxley also suggest that by 1200 most or perhaps all of the land recorded under Serlo de Burci's Ragiol in the Domesday Book had passed to Flaxley Abbey.

We know something of the families of this early period, with the Hosates probably the earliest known inhabitants of Nempnett.

However, at this distance in time sources of information are scarce, incomplete and sometimes contradictory, and this part of the story of the history of the parish is never likely to be written in great detail. More likely are a series of tantalising insights into how various important individuals' lives crossed in some way with the history of the parish.

Regilbury Manor 1537-1860

INTRODUCTION

This is the second of two chapters that deal with the history of the ownership of the Manor of Regilbury. Chapter 6 discussed what is known about the Manor from the Domesday Book through the period when it was under the control of Flaxley Abbey. Details of that period are relatively sketchy, but much more is known about Regilbury Manor than many other local manors. For the period covered by this chapter, 1537-1860, detailed information is available on the chain of ownership and the individuals who were Lord of the Manor, although there remain some areas where information is incomplete or contradictory.

THE KINGSTONS

The Abbey of Flaxley was suppressed in 1536 and in the following year the Abbey and its estates were granted to Sir William Kingston by a patent dated 26 March 1537. This grant included the "Manor of Rochelbury in the County of Somerset... together with all other rights pertaining thereto." Sir William Kingston was a close friend of Henry VIII and a Knight of his Privy Chamber. He was stated to be foremost amongst all Courtiers and positions of trust, one of the best Captains at Sea, and one of the most skilful commanders on land. He is said to have had an endearing but unfeeling personality and to have constantly flattered the King. He died in the street of Painswick, his home village in Gloucestershire, in 1540 when a sudden fit overcame him.

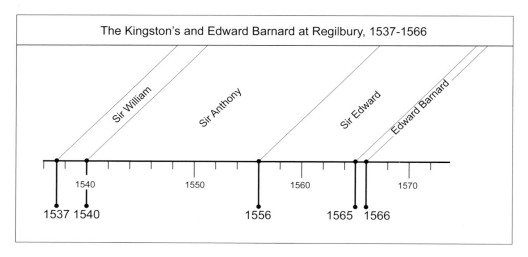

Figure 60: Regilbury timeline 1537-1566, the Kingstons and Edward Barnard

Sir Williams' possessions, including Flaxley and Rochelbury Manor, were passed to his son Sir Anthony Kingston, in two patents dated 1543 and 1544. In the 1544 grant the Manor of Rochelbury is valued at £23 with a yearly rent of £20.[1] During 1548-49 Sir Anthony was Provost Marshall of the Army and took an active part in crushing rebels in the West of England, for which he became famous as "the Terrible Provost Marshall" on account of his cruelty. In 1556 he was involved in a plot to rob the Exchequer to fund a rebellion, and was summoned to trial in London. He died on the way to London on 14 April 1556, some say of a heart attack caused by fear, others say by suicide by way of deliberately drowning himself in the Thames at Wallingford.

Regilbury Manor then passed into the hands of Edward Kingston, the son of Sir Anthony, who then sold it in 1565 to Edward Barnard Esq. The following year Barnard sold Regilbury to Edward Baber Esq., Sergeant at-Law. The ownership of Regilbury over this period is summarised in Figure 60.

THE BABERS

The Babers were Lords of the Manor of Regilbury from 1566 to 1714 - see Figure 61. They were a prosperous family at this time, with major land holdings in Chew Magna, Aldwick, Bath, Timsbury, Corston, Newton St Loe and elsewhere. The Baber

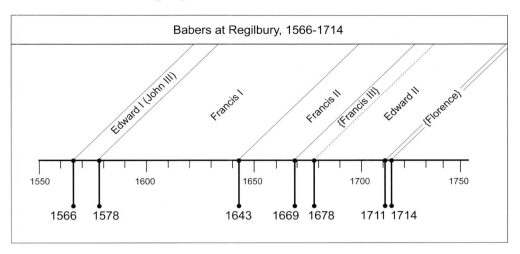

Babers at Regilbury, 1566-1714

Edward I (John III)   Francis I   Francis II   {Francis III}   Edward II   {Florence}

1550   1600   1650   1700   1750

1566   1578   1643   1669   1678   1711   1714

Figure 61: Regilbury timeline 1566-1714, the Babers

family tree has been extensively researched by the Baber Family Tree Society, and Vera Baber's 35-year study of the family worldwide has resulted in a well-documented history for all of the English-descended lines plus others in Australia, New Zealand, South Africa, India, Malaysia, British Honduras, and the United States of America. At the time of writing the family tree included 21,620 individuals in 8,448 family groups.

The earliest ancestor recorded in the Baber family tree is John, a tenant farmer from Chew Stoke, who died 7 January 1527. His will, which was proved on 14 February 1527, includes a gift to St. Mary's Church Nempnett, along with gifts to the churches of Chew Magna, Chew Stoke, and Winford, and the cathedral at Wells.

John's descendants are shown in Figure 62. He married twice, first Alice Adams, and then Isabel (surname unknown). It appears that by both marriages he had a son called John, that by Alice Adams being known as John the Elder of Regilbury, and that by Isabel, John the Younger of Chew Stoke. John the Elder also married twice. His first wife was Agnes Willett of Butcombe, and they are known to have had four sons, the youngest of which, Edward, was to purchase the Manor of Regilbury. John the Elder had further offspring by his second wife Mary, including Thomas, Margaret and Joan.

John the Elder of Regilbury seems to have been a tenant farmer at Regilbury, since in his will he passes on to his youngest

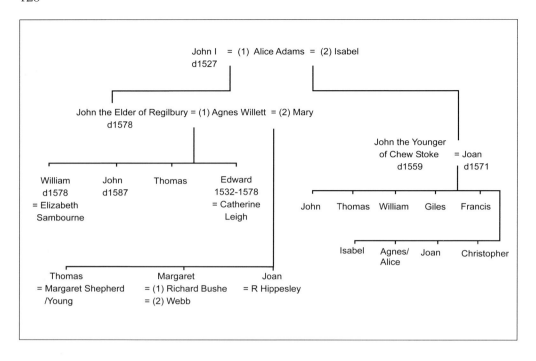

Figure 62: The Baber family tree, 1527-1578

son Edward the leases on Regilbury "for two lives and one life afterwards in reversion in another copy according unto the custom of the Manor".[2] It is not clear whether John was a tenant at Regilbury before his son Edward bought the Manor in 1566.

John the Elder of Regilbury died in 1578. In his will he asks to be buried in Nempnett Church, and leaves money to the churches of Nempnett, Blagdon, Winford and Butcombe and to the cathedral at Wells. John had begun to acquire his own lands, for in addition to the leases on Regilbury he also leaves to Edward "all the lands late of Paul Taverner in Wrington and in Bristol.... [which] I bought .. and paid for .. with mine own goods". He makes his two eldest sons, John and William, his executors, but leaves the bulk of his inheritance to the youngest son Edward. Quite what the relationship between his children was we will never know but his will contains the following passage:

> I mean not, nor will not, that the said John Baber [my son] neither William Baber by any means of executorship to trouble my son Edward their brother neither his son or

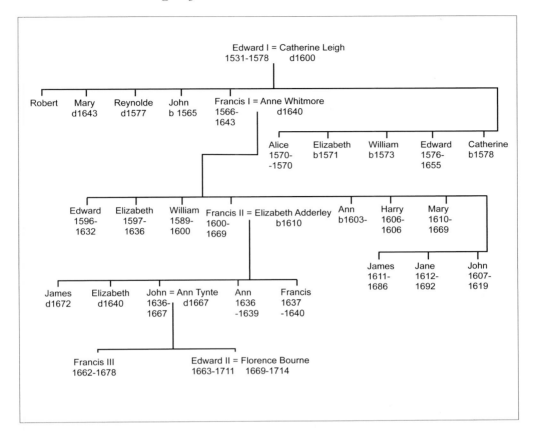

Figure 63: The Baber family tree, 1531-1714

heirs male, but shall quietly suffer them without any trouble in anywise of the said John or William about the lands of the Manor of Regilbury or of any part of the lands late of Paul Taverner but I will the said John and William suffer their brother Edward and his issue male quietly to enjoy the said lands without any trouble. And in like manner I will not that my son Edward Baber trouble but quietly suffer his brothers John and William my executors. Son Edward I heartily desire you for God's sake to be good and friendly to your brothers and sisters with comfort in all causes of right and equity as truth, grace and honesty belongeth among you. So I desire God to bless you with his grace and brotherly love the one unto the other among you.[3]

Edward Baber, often referred to as Edward Baber Sergeant-at-Law, was the youngest son of John the Elder of Regilbury and Agnes Willett, and was born in 1531 or 1532. He attended Lincoln's Inn in London, where he trained and then practised as a lawyer. In 1560 he made an advantageous marriage to Catherine Leigh, the third daughter of Sir Thomas Leigh who was a prominent mercer and former Lord Mayor of London. They had ten children, as shown in Figure 63.

In 1570 Edward became a Justice of the Peace in Somerset, and in 1571 he was appointed as Recorder in Bath and so became one of the two Members of Parliament for Bath for the years 1571 and 1572. The following year he was appointed a Governor of Lincoln's Inn; in 1574 he became a Justice of the Peace for Middlesex and in 1577 was raised to Sergeant-at-Law.

He acquired extensive lands in Somerset, including the Manors of Aldwick and Regilbury and by 1573 he had property in London and Bristol. It seems likely, although there are no details, that Edward rebuilt or improved the main house at Regilbury, since a later painting suggests a structure dating to about this period. His main residence in Somerset appears to have been Aldwick.

Regilbury Manor must have been an important place at around this time, since it is included on Saxton's 1575 Map of Somerset. It is spelt Regilburye and the symbol used suggests a manor or a house rather than a church; an extract of Saxton's map is shown in Figure 64. It is also worth noting that just to the west of Regilburye is shown another house named Brodweldowne; this may be an early spelling or version of what we now call Broadfield Down and this place may be the precursor of today's Butcombe Court (see Chapter 9).

In 1574 Edward Baber was granted a coat of arms as shown in Figure 65 and Plate 13. The formal description is as follows:

> Baber, Edward, of Regelbery, Somerset, Esq. Grant of a crest to be borne by the descendants of his father John Baber, by Robert Cooke, dated Jan. 1574. The arms, argent on a fess gu. three hawks' heads erased of the first.[4]

The heraldic terms are explained thus: the colour of the background is argent (silver), which is said to represent purity innocence, beauty or gentleness, on this there is a red strip (the term fess being a strip, and gu. an abbreviation for gule the colour red). There are three hawks heads on the red strip which

Figure 64: Extract from Saxton's 1575 map of Somerset showing Regilbury

are described as "erased" which means having the appearance of being forcibly torn off, leaving jagged or uneven ends (rather than cleanly cut); red is said to signify military fortitude and magnanimity, and hawks one who feared not to signal his approach in either peace or war.[5]

Edward died on 23 September 1578, aged about 47, and is buried in St Andrew's Church Chew Magna, where the Baber Monument was erected by his son Francis in his honour, see Plates 12-15.

Edward's will is a lengthy document, running to over 4,500 words.[6] It is also rather poignant, since at the time of writing his sons were still young boys, Francis being about 12 at the time of his death and William about 5. He urges his executors to have special regard to the "bringing up of my children in virtue and in learning, or in some good service or occupation according to their several dispositions" and he says "I commit them principally to the gracious and merciful tuition of Almighty God to remain and be in the rule and governance of the said Catherine my loving wife their mother".

Edward first leaves what appear to be a series of tenancies to his sons. He leaves to Robert "the manor house, demesne and farm of Aldwick with the appurtenances in Blagdon in the said County of Somerset late in the tenancy or occupation of one Richard Draper or of his assigns, and all the houses, lands meadows, pastures, feedings, woods, underwoods and commons to the same farm belonging". He leaves to William "all that my tenement and toft called Hill House with appurtenances situate, lying and being in Blagdon aforesaid late in the tenure and occupation of one John Elcock Gent. deceased or of his assigns and all houses, lands meadows, pastures, feedings, woods, underwoods and commons to the same tenement and toft". And he leaves to Francis Baber "my messuage and tenement situate lying and being at Lye alias Leigh in the parish of Wrington in the said County of Somerset late in the possession of one Robert Yeeles, and all the houses, orchards, gardens, lands, meadows, pastures, feedings, woods, underwoods, commons and hereditaments thereunto belonging".

Edward then leaves to Francis "the Lordship, farm and grange of Regilbury Manor", "my lease in the parsonage of Nempnett" and also "my books which I shall have in Middlesex and Chew in Somerset at the time of my decease". His wife Catherine inherits the Manor of Chew Magna and "all other things which I bought of Sir Ambrose Jermyn, knight".

It is clear that in the 50 years or so since 1527 when the first John Baber of Chew Stoke died, the Baber's had become a rich family, and one with good connections too, for Edward makes the overseers of his will Sir William Cordell, Knight, Master of the Rolls of the High Court of the country and Thomas Bromley, Esquire, the Queen Majesty's Solicitor General.

Francis, Edward's son, is thought to have been born (on maybe baptised?) 25 August 1566 in St. James, Clerkenwell, London. On 24 July 1595 he married Ann Whitmore, daughter of William Whitmore of Apley, Shropshire, and brother of Sir George Whitmore of Balmes, Middlesex, the staunch Royalist and Lord Mayor of London 1631-12. They had nine children. Francis was Justice of the Peace under three sovereigns, Elizabeth I, James I and Charles I, and was High Sheriff of Somerset in 1611. He appears to have lived mainly at the Manor of Chew Magna, which he owned along with Regilbury. He died on 9 September 1643, aged 65, with his son Francis II inheriting Regilbury Manor. A window in his honour is to be found in Bath Abbey.

Francis II was born about 6 July 1600 in Chew Magna, Somerset. He gained a degree from Oxford University in 1616, was known as a Doctor of Civil Law, and married Elizabeth, daughter of John Adderley Esq., on 9 April 1634 in South

Figure 65: The Baber coat of arms

Mimms, Middlesex. Francis II appears to have lived at Regilbury from 1654 or thereabouts.

A letter that Francis II wrote from at Regilbury, dated 18 February 1660, survives at the Bristol Record Office.[7] The letter is to Sir Thomas Bridges and Hugh Smith Esq., two of the Deputy Lieutenants of the Militia of Somerset, and concerns military service. Francis notes that he is at present rated to provide two horses and riders, and asks firstly whether his obedience is to Capt. Bampfield at Chewton or Sir William Basset at Felton Down from both of whom he has received summons, and secondly, that the assessment be reduced since his estates were much diminished since his father's time. An extract of the letter is shown in Figure 66.

Francis II died in 1669 aged 69, and is buried in Abbot Seabroke Chapel in Gloucester Cathedral. His first heir was his son John, who was born in 1636, and married Ann or Barbara Tynte, daughter of Colonel John Tynte of Chelvey Court. However, John died in 1667 or 1668 (before his father), aged just 31, and the inheritance passed to Francis' grandsons. Thus, Francis III came into the inheritance on the death of Francis II in 1669, but he died under age in 1678 and was succeeded by his brother Edward II.

Edward II, the great-great grandson of Edward Sergeant of Arms, was the last Baber to own Regilbury. He was born about 20 January 1663 or 1664 in Chew Magna, matriculated from Oxford University in 1680 at age 16, and married Florence, daughter and heiress of Roger Bourne Esq. of Gothelney in the parish of Charlinch, at St Vedast, Foster Lane, London on 24 June 1687. According the Strachey manuscripts Edward II "repaired, rebuilt, enlarged and beautified the old House" and "lived there in great splendour." St. David Kemeys-Tynte's history of Regilbury includes a reproduction of an oil painting by an unknown artist, showing Regilbury House and the surrounding outbuildings and countryside at around 1700 and this is shown in Figure 67. A more detailed sketch of what the house itself might have looked like, based on the painting and the work of Roger Gallannaugh, is shown in Figure 68.[8]

Edward II died in 1711, by coincidence at the same age of 47 as his great-great grandfather Edward I Sergeant at-Law. Edward II left no offspring and bequeathed his estates to his wife Florence. His will is as follows:

> Edward Baber, of Regilbury, in Nempnett, Somerset, England. Jan. 8, 1705/6. Proved by Florence Baber, May 5, 1711. To be buried in the vault made by my ancestors in Chew Magna Church. To my wife Florence Baber all my Manors, Lordships, etc., of Chew Magna, Regilbury, Pensford, Axbridge, my Kings lands in Nempnett, & all my messuages in Wrington, Berington, etc., the Rectory of Norton Hawkfield, and all my goods, &c.

This will raises a question regarding Nempnett, namely where are the "Kings lands." The fact that it is mentioned separately from the Manor of Regilbury may be significant, and it may refer to the lands on Kingsdown which at that time were still common land.

Florence Baber survived her husband by only three years, and died in 1714. Her will, proved on 2 September 1715, is as follows:

> Florence Baber of Regelbury, County Somerset, Widow. Will dated 3 April, 1713 To kinsman Sir Halswell Tynte, Bart. and his heirs the Mayors and Lordships of Chew Magna, Regelbury, Pensford and Axbridge, land called Kingslands in Nempnett, with the tithes etc. of Nempnett, Trubwell, Wrington, Berrington and Blagdon had from testatrix late husband Edward Baber Esq. To Mr. Joseph Yate £500 borrowed. Kinswoman Martha Stocker, daughter of Joseph Stocker grocer by Martha his late wife £2000 to remain at interest until she is 21. Estates in remainder to testatrix next brother John Tynte and after to her younger brother Charles Tynte. Kinsman Thomas Bourne Gent.

Figure 66: Extract from Francis Baber's 1660 letter

son of Edmund Bourne late of Road Esq., deceased and his heirs the Manor of Gothelney which came to testatrix from Roger Bourne Esq., her late father; with reminder to John Bourne son of Henry Bourne late of Charlinch, Gent. dec. Kinswoman Mrs. Martha and Mrs. Mary Hooke each £100. Kinswoman Sarah, Elizabeth, Susanna, and Ann Bourne daughters of Gilbert Bourne Esq. dec. £100 each. Cousin Mr. Robert Knight and his sister Mrs. Ann Knight, £100 each. To Eleanor Baker of Bristol spinster £100. To aunt Mrs. Frances Butler wife of Mr. Robert Butler, Minister of God's word £50. Sarah Bourne relict of Henry Bourne late of Charlinch £50. To the parish of Chew Magna £100.

Later references suggest that Francis Baber's will included a gift to the parish of Nempnett Thrubwell. Thus, the Report of the Commissioners for Inquiring Concerning Charities has the following entry under the Parish of Nempnett for a "Florence Baber's Charity":

REGILBURY HOUSE, SOMERSET.
(Circa 1700).

Figure 67: Oil painting of Regilbury House c. 1700

"By the last will of Madam Florence Baber, deceased, bearing [the] date the 3 April 1713, was given the parish the sum of £50 to be placed out at interest, and the increase and profits thereof to be employed in binding out poor children apprentice to some honest calling the same to remain for ever."

However it appears that this gift was "lost" since the Charities Report goes on to note that in the returns made to Parliament in 1786 under the Act usually called Gilbert's Act, the following statement is made relating to Florence Baber's request:

"Not paid since 1759, both principal and interest refused by John Summers; parish expended £10 18s [£10.90p] in endeavouring to obtain it, but without effect. Mr Summers' effects being in Chancery, it is doubtful whether recoverable."

The Charities Report then notes that nothing has been since obtained under the will above mentioned.

It is the generally accepted version of events that Florence Baber's will marked the end of the period when the Babers were Lords of the Manor at Regilbury and that there was then a straightforward transfer of ownership to the Tyntes, later called the Kemeys-Tyntes.

*Figure 68: Sketch
of Regilbury House
c. 1700*

However, some accounts say that the Somers Family were at about this time involved in some way at Regilbury. A note in Somerset & Dorset Notes & Queries in 1899, attributed to D.K.T, probably St. David Kemeys-Tynte, says a John Somers lived at Regilbury Court and died there in 1778. And in the same journal a note by R.G.B. in 1920 says:

> "Regilbury Court came into the possession of the Somers Family in the early part of the 18th century. John Bartlett, Esq. (born at Corton, Somerset), Mayor and Alderman of Bristol, in his will dated 16 January 1747-8, appoints his brother-in-law John Somers, Esq., of Regilbury to be one of his executors."

The same article has a list of eight entries in the Nempnett Parish Registers for Somers between 1726 and 1785.

The historical records of Regilbury Manor provide no evidence that the Somers were ever Lords of the Manor, but there were tenants named Somers and Summers on the estate in the mid- to late-18th century.[9] The entry in the Charities report that John Summers had control over Florence Baber's bequest to the parish suggests some link between Florence Baber and the Somers or Summers family. However, the exact role the Somers family played in the affairs of Regilbury and Nempnett at about this time remains unclear.

THE TYNTES (KEMEYS-TYNTES)

The Tyntes are an ancient family, thought to date back to at least 1192 and to have been in Somerset since the 13th century. They are known to have been in Wraxall in 1327 and to have bought the Manor of Chelvey in 1619. Later in the 17th century John Tynte married Jane Halswell, sole heiress of the Halswells, and so moved to Halswell House, Goathurst, about 6 km from Bridgwater. John's son Halswell was made a baronet in 1674 and he rebuilt the main house in 1689 in grand style.

The association between the Tyntes and Regilbury began in 1714; the Timeline of the Tyntes as Lords of the Manor is shown in Figure 69 and the associated family tree in Figure 70. The first Tynte Lord of the Manor was Sir Halswell, the third Baronet and eldest son of Sir John Tynte, the second Baronet of Halswell (who died in 1710 and had married Jane Kemeys heiress of the Baronetcy of Cefn Mably). Sir Halswell, born 15 November 1705, graduated from New College Oxford and was returned unopposed as Tory Member of Parliament for Bridgwater 1727-1730. On 28 September 1727 he married Mary, daughter and heiress of John Waters of Brecon, and they had two daughters, but both died young and at the time of his death on 12 November 1730 aged 25 he was without heirs.

Sir Halswell was succeeded by his brother, the Rev Sir John Tynte, born 27 March 1707, the fourth Baronet of Halswell, who was Rector of Goathurst. He never married and on his death on 15 August 1740 aged 33 he was succeeded by his brother Charles, who used the hyphenated surname Kemeys-Tynte.

Sir Charles Kemeys-Tynte, born 19 May 1710, thus became the fifth Baronet of Halswell, and on his mother's death in 1747 succeeded also to the Baronetcy of Cefn Mably. He unsuccessfully contested Glamorgan seat as a Tory in 1745 but was later elected MP for Monmouth 1745-7 and for Somerset 1747-74. He left one of the finest landscaped gardens in the country at Goathurst, which included a temple dedicated to Robin Hood, a Rotunda and a Druid Temple. He married Anne daughter and co-heir of Rev Thomas Busby in March 1737-8. On his death on 25 August 1785 aged 75 Sir Charles had no heirs, the Baronetcies of Halswell and Cefn Mably both became extinct and after the death of his wife Lady Ann in 1798 his estates devolved to his niece Jane Hassell, the only daughter of his sister Jane's marriage to Major Russhie Hassell.

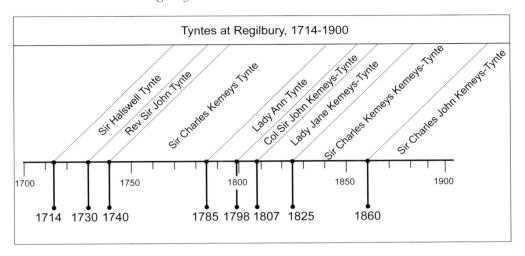

Figure 69: Regilbury timeline 1714-1900, the Tyntes

Jane Hassell had married Colonel John Johnson of the 1st Foot Guards and Groom of the Bedchamber and Controller of the Prince of Wales (afterwards George IV), and son of Lt-Gen Johnson of Burhill, Surrey and Glaston, Rutland. Col John and Jane then assumed by Royal Licence the name and arms of Kemeys-Tynte. He died in 1807 and she in 1825, leaving two daughters, Jane and Anne Georgina, and one son Charles Kemeys, the latter inheriting their estates.

Charles Kemeys Kemeys-Tynte, born 29 May 1778, was MP for Bridgwater 1820-37 and Colonel of the West Somerset Yeomen. He was also Provincial Grand Master of the Freemasons for Somerset 1820-60, during which time he is said to have devoted himself whole-heartedly to the cause of freemasonry. On 25 April 1798 he married Anne, widow of Thomas Lewis of St. Pierre, Monmouth and daughter of Rev. Thomas Leyson, Vicar of Bassaleg, Monmouth. In 1845 Col. Charles Kemeys Kemeys-Tynte was declared by the Committee of Privileges of the House of Lords to be the co-heir to the barony of Wharton but no further proceedings were taken. He died on 28 November 1860. A copy of his portrait from the Braikenridge Collection is shown in Figure 71.

Charles was succeeded by his son Charles John Kemeys-Tynte, who was born 1799 and died 1882. He was Colonel of the Royal Glamorgan Infantry, MP for West Somerset 1832-37 and for Bridgwater 1847-65. He too was a Freemason and was

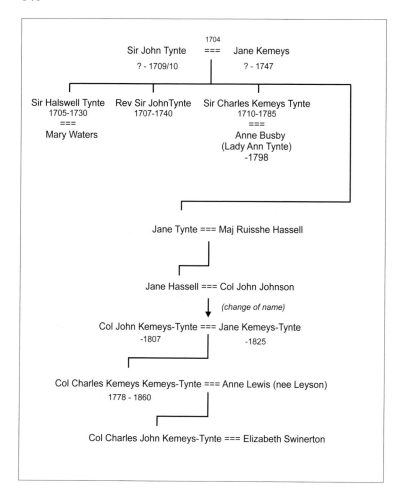

Figure 70: Tynte family tree 1704-1900

appointed Provincial Grand Master for Monmouthshire in 1831, although it is said he subsequently gave practically no time to these duties.

At some time at the beginning of the period when Regilbury was in the hands of the Tyntes the main house became the retirement residence of Sir William Wyndham, arguably the most famous Nempnett resident. William Wyndham, 1687-1740, entered parliament in 1710 and became Secretary-at-War in the Tory ministry in 1712 and Chancellor of the Exchequer in 1713. He was closely associated with Lord Bollingbroke and was privy to attempts made to bring about a Jacobite restoration on the death of Queen Anne. Under George I Wyndham was leader

COLONEL CHARLES KEMEYS KEMEYS TYNTE,

of Halswell, *& Cevenmelly,*
in the County of Somerset, *in the County of Glamorgan.*

Dedicated by permission to the Freemasons of Somerset,
by their obedient Servant *J. E. Ford.*

ENTERED AT STATIONERS HALL.

Figure 71: Portrait of Col Charles Kemeys Kemeys-Tynte

of the opposition in the House of Commons, and a strong supporter of the High Church and Tory principles. He died at Wells 17 June 1740.

It would appear that after the tenancy of Regilbury House to William Wyndham expired "the old house lapsed again into decay, was dismantled and partly pulled down, and what remained of it turned into a farm house." A painting from the Braikenridge Collection believed to date to 1846 and said to show the ruins of part of Regilbury Court is shown in Figure 72. Some years before, in 1832, the Rev John Skinner visited Regilbury, after his work at Fairy's Toot. In his diary for 21 August 1822 he says:

> Being anxious to visit the ruins of an old mansion at
> Regelsbury....we walked thither, under the escort of two
> of the workmen who had assisted us in our operations at
> Fairy Toot; a part only of the building now remains, and
> the free stone of the windows having been for the most
> part removed, it is not easy to determine on the date of its
> erection; probably about the times of Elizabeth, or James
> the First; not but what a more ancient residence might
> have occupied the spot, even as the Roman times; since it
> is quite contiguous to the Portway from Nemnet.[10]

Today Regilbury Court is largely a modern building, but some portions of the old house remain, see Plates 17 and 18. The site is listed on the current Sites and Monuments Records, where it is described as "16th-17th Century with some 18th Century alterations, a surviving portion of a much larger house, built in the reign of Elizabeth I and enlarged and altered in the late 17th Century, partly demolished and turned into a farmhouse in the late 18th Century". Within the garden of the house is what appears to be the beginning of a tunnel, about 2m in circumference, and this could be part of the basis for the locally held belief that there is a secret tunnel running between Regilbury Court and Butcombe Court, a distance of some 1.5km. However, there are many examples of such "secret tunnels" in folklore, usually linking places of local importance, but few prove to have any basis in fact. Also of interest is the man-made lake just to the east of the house and in Winford parish, which recent excavations proved to have a cobbled bottom. Local belief is that this was used to breed fish for the table; the lake is drawn in pencil on the 1778 map of Regilbury Court (see Plate 16).

CONCLUSIONS

In the period after the dissolution of the monasteries there is much more information about the line of ownership of Regilbury Manor. After a brief period in the hands of the colourful Kingston family, Regilbury became part of the extensive Baber family estate. Many Babers lived at or owned Regilbury, and

Figure 72: Painting of the ruins of Regilbury Court c. 1846

there is some material from this period at the Somerset Record Office. The transfer of ownership to the Tyntes linked Regilbury to another well-known Somerset family, and by good fortune a fairly extensive archive of papers from Regilbury is held at the Somerset Record Office, including the court roll of the Manor of Regilbury, which appears to be largely unstudied.

Despite the increasing availability of manuscript sources, many uncertainties remain. There is a difference between ownership and occupation, and in many periods it is not clear who, if anyone, actually lived in Regilbury, and when the buildings fell derelict and were refurbished. Similarly there is some confusion over the connection of the Summers or Somers family with Regilbury. Other issues not addressed here include the origins of Regilbury Park Farm and the supposed medieval deer park (see Chapter 5). The next chapter addresses the specific question of the geography of Regilbury Manor, that is to say, where exactly its lands were.

8   The Geography of Regilbury Manor 1730

INTRODUCTION

The previous two chapters have discussed the history of the ownership of Regilbury Manor, which can be traced in some detail from the Domesday Book through to the present day. However, much less is known about the geography of the Manor, that is to say, where exactly its holdings were to be found. Indeed there is much confusion and uncertainty about this. It is often assumed that the Manor's lands were centred on the hamlet of Ridgehill or Regil in the parish of Winford, some 1 km or so to the south-east of Regilbury Court. In his *The History and Antiquities of the County of Somerset* published in 1791 and widely regarded as one of the most authoritative works on the history of the area, Collinson speaks of "the village of Nempnett [being] an appendage to the Manor of Regilbury" suggesting that much of the Manor's lands were in Nempnett parish. Some other works appear to confuse Regilbury with the hamlet of Redhill some 3km to the east in Wrington parish.

The aim of this chapter is to recreate the geography of the Manor of Regilbury as it was in 1730. The starting point is a survey of the Manor by William Williams in that year, which records a total area of just over 1,230 acres divided between 30 holdings. For each holding is given a detailed acreage, the current tenant, the rent, the lives for which the tenancy holds and the heriot due on the change of tenancy. Intriguingly in the ledger that records these details there is also a small coloured box for each holding which looks like it might be a key for a map that accompanied the survey, but if such a map existed it does not appear to have survived. The survey is held in the Somerset Record Office at DD/S/WH 224.

The main conclusion of this chapter is that much of the parish of Nempnett Thrubwell was part of the estate of the Manor of Regilbury in 1730, about 780 acres of the parish, or in very rough terms about half. This is, as far as I am aware, the first detailed analysis which backs up Collinson's statement of the importance of Regilbury Manor in the affairs of the parish and quantifies the extent of Regilbury's holdings in the parish for a particular date.

The sections that follow record in detail the steps of the analysis which led to these conclusions. There is much detail here, provided for anyone interested in pursuing the matter further, but many, I suspect, will find it somewhat dry. Such readers may wish to peruse the maps and skip to the final section which draws together the main findings.

DATA SOURCES AND METHOD

To discover the geography of these holdings a number of sources were consulted covering the period 1714-1841. First, there are a large number of documents stored at the Somerset Record Office that relate to the Manor of Regilbury during the Tyntes' period of ownership, which include rental accounts and bundles of miscellaneous deeds, the main ones of which are DD/S/WH 180-231, DD/FS 16/4/1, DD/RN 43 and 62, DD/BRC 17. Some of these deeds contain listings of field names, which are especially important for mapping purposes, while others allow the tenancy of various holdings to be traced through time. There are a small number of deeds that relate to the earlier period of Baber ownership.

A second important source is Volume 1 of the Report of the Commissioners regarding the Charitable Institutions in Bristol, edited by Thomas John Manchee and published in 1831, henceforth referred to as Bristol Charities (1831). A considerable amount of the land belonging to Regilbury Manor was bought by, or given to, Alderman Henry Bengough of Bristol around 1818 and then held in a charitable trust in which Trinity Hospital had a reversionary interest. The Bristol Charities publication contains detailed listings of this land including field names.

Thirdly, the Tithe Maps of 1841 provide the basis for the mapping of the holdings. The Tithe Maps and Apportionments

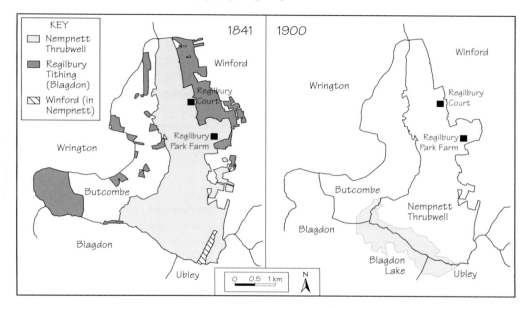

Figure 73: Regilbury Court and parish boundaries 1841 and 1900

for the parish of Nempnett, the Tithing of Regilbury (then in the parish of Blagdon) and the separate return for the lands of Charles Kemeys Kemeys-Tynte Esq.

After these various sources had been gathered and analysed the objective was to collate the relevant information by holding, and, as far as was possible, to derive for each of the 30 holdings a continuous run of tenants' names from 1714 to 1841, together with a list of field names that define the geographical location of the holding. The degree of difficulty of this task varied between holdings, as did the methods of working and the degree of success. Of the 1730 survey only one holding has proved to be impossible to identify and of the others about 1141 acres (about 93% of the total area) have been mapped with some degree of confidence and 1189 acres (97%) have been allocated to parishes. The next sections describe in detail how each holding was identified and present maps of their extent.

HOLDINGS OF REGILBURY MANOR, 1730

Table 2 lists the 30 holdings as they were recorded in the 1730 survey, together with the tenants' names and the area in acres, rods, and perches. (There are four rods to an acre, 40 perches to a rod; some tenants are known only by their surname.) The ordering of the holdings is as given in the 1730 survey. It became apparent in the progress of this research that the ordering is significant, since it represents a geographical pattern, with holdings that are nearby on the ground also being nearby in the survey.

Figure 73 shows the location of Regilbury Court and Regilbury Park Farm and the parish boundaries of 1841 and 1900. The parishes in 1841 are complex. Of particular note is Regilbury Tithing, a part of Blagdon parish, which was made up of a block of land around Regilbury Court, a few scattered fields to the south around Stroud, a larger number of scattered fields in Butcombe parish and another block of land further west around Aldwick. Similarly, Nempnett Thrubwell included some scattered fields around Stroud and the small plot of Butcombe Mill, while a strip of land around Henmarsh Farm was an outlying part of Winford.

By 1900 a process of "consolidation" had resulted in the "modern" parishes made up of contiguous blocks of land (see Chapter 1). Figure 73 reminds us that the neat and tidy pattern of parishes we see today was not always the case and explains why there are many references to Blagdon parish in the documents of Regilbury Manor, which refer to the Regilbury Tithing of the 18th and 19th centuries.

Park Domain (Figure 74, top left)
The estimated location of the Park Domain holding is derived largely from a plan and valuation of Regilbury Court, Park Farm and Crudwells Tenement, shown in Plate 16, which is dated 1778 and includes a detailed sketch map giving field names and areas, and which can be accurately cross-referenced to the Tithe Maps of 1841 – the plan is held at SRO at DD/S/WH 199. When Crudwells tenement is removed (see below) a total of 366 acres remains, and this is the area mapped.

In the 1730 Survey (Table 2) the area of the Park Domain is given as just over 293 acres, but if it assumed that the 44 acres "in hand" are also part of the Park Domain the mapped area of 366 acres in Figure 74 compares to 338 acres in the 1730 survey. The discrepancy of 28 acres may be because the Kingdown Tinings (18 acres) and Crudwell Tining (6 acres) holdings that are listed separately in the 1730 survey had, by 1778, been incorporated into the Park Domain.

	Name	Tenant	A	R	P
	to hand		44	0	31
1	Park Domain	Abross Marshall	293	3	11
2	Regil Town Tenement	George Morgan	69	0	24
3	Crudwells Tenement	Richard Hanan	43	1	1
4	Crudwell House	In hand	1	0	14
5	East Kingdown Tenement	Walter Webb	54	2	39
6	Kingdown Tinings	John Young	18	0	39
7	Crudwell Tining	Lane	6	2	36
8	Broadway Down Tenement In Butcombe	George Collier	5	1	38
9	West Kingdown Tenement	Ephrim Clement	44	2	6
10	Merry Fields Tenement	John Ford	37	0	35
11	Stroud Batch Tenement	Nath Pean	17	3	23
12	Mid Stroud Tenement	Mary Morgan	35	1	21
13	Son Stroud Tenement	John Holebrook	2	1	36
14	Church House Tenement Nempnett	Edward Saunders	52	0	19
15	New House Tenement	Sarah Hipsley	15	1	30
16	Roofless Tenement, Now House in Nempnett	Sarah Hipsley	8	0	27
17	Pigg Stie Hole	Sarah Cook	18	3	22
18	Pigg Stie Cottage 40' by 40'	Sarah Cook	0		
19	East House Tenement	Isaac Hort	66	0	15
20	Home Tenement, Nempnett	Isaac Hort	79	1	30
21	Hills Tenement, Nempnett	Isaac Hort	15	3	17
22	Cuckoos Nest	Richard West	1	0	20
23	Rowlings and Bayleys Place Nempnett	Thomas Beal	95	1	13
24	Webbs Tenement		70	1	18
25	Thatchers Tenement	Richard West	58	0	31
26	Roofless Tenement	Cattcutt	16	3	24
27	Sands Tenement	Hill	35	1	11
28	Roofless Tenement	Hill	6	2	28
29	Wades Roofless Tenement	Collins	14	0	27
30	Butcombe Mill Tenement	Vowles	1	3	18
	Total		1230	0	24

Table 2: Holdings of Regilbury Manor 1730

Regil Town Tenement (Figure 74, top right)

The 1730 survey has the occupier of this tenement as George Morgan, with an annual rent of £1 1s 8d and dues of 4 cocks or hens. These details of the rent and dues match the deeds of DD/S/WH 181 No 20, which include a lease with George

Morgan, dated 1739. Although in these deeds this holding is described simply as "in Nempnett and Blagdon" it appears very likely this is the Regil Town Tenement. These deeds include a list of field names with approximate acreages.

The Tithe Map Apportionment for Regilbury Tithing has a set of entries under the heading "The Regil Town Estate," which is owned by Charles Kemeys Kemeys-Tynte Esq., then the owner Regilbury. About a half of these fields could be matched with some degree of certainty to the names listed in DD/S/WH 181 No 20. As this estate is of roughly the right size, and since the deeds of DD/S/WH 181 No 20 show the estate appears not to have changed through the period 1694 to 1803, this was judged to be the Regil Town Tenement. The main residence of this holding is Regilbury Farm in the main street of Regil village. The mapped area is *c.* 63 acres compared to *c.* 69 in the 1730 survey.

3. Crudwells Tenement (Figure 74, lower left)
The 1730 survey has this tenement as rented to Richard Hannam with a rent of £1, and this matches DD/S/WH 181 No 19 which is a lease for "Criddles – four pieces of land" to Richard Hannam dated 1733 with a rent of £1. Inspection of the sketch map in SRO DD/S/WH 199 (see Plate 16) that includes Crudwells Tenement suggests that four adjacent fields which total *c.* 43 acres, three of which include the name Crudwell, are likely to make up this tenement, and these are mapped in Figure 74.

4. Crudwells House (not mapped)
The Tithe Map for Regilbury Tithing shows two buildings at the north-east corner of Crudwells tenement, on the south side of the cross-roads at Kingdown, and it seems that one of these houses with a curtilage of *c.* 0.2 acres, together with a small adjacent field to the south of *c.* 0.8 acres, would have made up this tenement. In 1919 the Manor of Regilbury still held cottages at the Kingdown crossroads (DD/QK 172).

5. East Kingdown Tenement (Figure 74, lower right)
The 1730 survey gives the area of this tenement as *c.* 54 acres, and other documents of the early 18th century give the rent as £1 0s 8d (DD/S/WH 223a and 228). These details match those of an unnamed holding in deeds DD/S/WH 181 No 28, which cover the period 1698-1790, suggesting these deeds are for East Kingdown tenement and that the tenement did not change

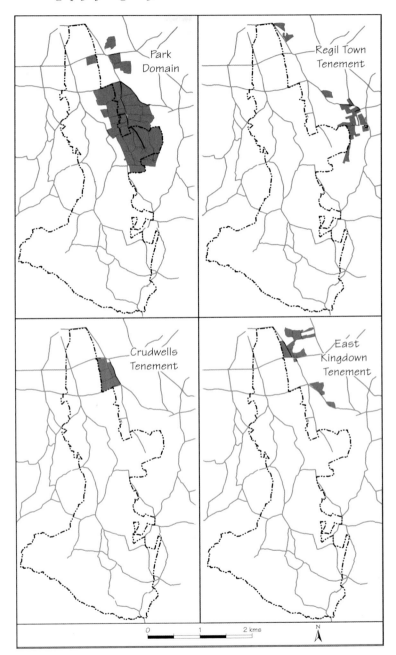

Figure 74: Regilbury Manor 1730:1 Park Domain and Regil Town, Crudwells and East Kingdown tenements

significantly over this period. There is a list of fields in these deeds and about half of these can be identified on the Regilbury Tithe Map, and those that can be identified all belong to the "East Kingdown Farm" estate listed in the Apportionment. Since that estate was owned by Charles Kemeys Kemeys-Tynte Esq. it seems reasonably certain that this is the East Kingdown Tenement of 1730. The main residence is the house on the north side of the Kingdown crossroads. The mapped area is *c.* 62 acres compared to *c.* 55 acres in the 1730 survey. The discrepancy may be due to Crudwell Tining being included in this estate.

6. Kingdown Tinings (not mapped)

The 1730 survey has this small holding of *c.* 18 acres in the tenancy of John Young, at a rent of 1s and with lives of Thomas and William Boles. A deed of Regilbury Manor dated 1793 (DD/RN/62 and DD/S/WH 180 Nos 7 and 10) is for a holding of *c.* 20 acres, with a rent of 1s and a previous tenant named as John Bowles (perhaps a descendant of the Boles mentioned in 1730) and this is tentatively identified as the Kingdown Tining holding of 1730.

This holding is described in deed DD/S/WH 180 as "two parcels of land on Kingdown Hill or Common, on the north side of the road from Winford to Wrington, of 8 and 12 acres." The most likely location would seem to be in the extreme north of the parish of Nempnett just to the west of the northernmost part of East Kingdown Tenement, but a separate map of this holding has not been prepared.

7. Crudwell Tining (not mapped)

No further information has been found for this small holding of *c.* 6 acres, and its location is therefore unknown. However, the name suggests it will be close to, or associated in some way with, Crudwells Tenement, for example it may well be a piece of land on Kingdown common originally tied to the Crudwells tenement.

8. Broadway Down Tenement in Butcombe (not mapped)

Like Crudwell Tining, it has not been possible to determine with any accuracy the exact location of this holding of *c.* 5 acres, although the name suggests it is on the high ground at the very north of Butcombe parish, just west of where Kingdown Tinings were judged to be.

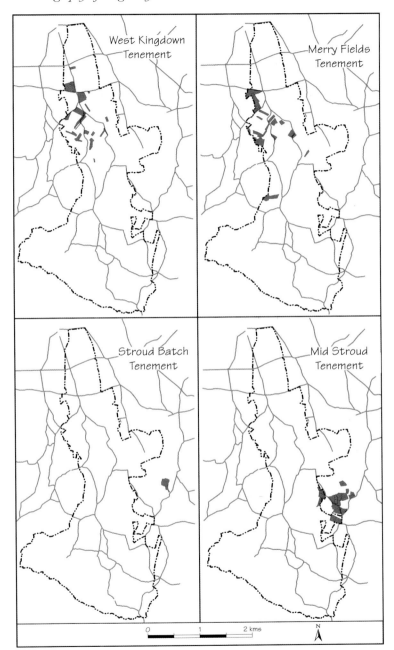

Figure 75: Regilbury Manor 1730: 2 West Kingdown, Merry Fields, Stroud Batch and Mid Stroud tenements

9. West Kingdown Tenement (Figure 75, top left)

In the 1730 survey this holding of *c.* 44 acres has a rental of 12s 8d. Two deeds (DD/RN 43) dated 1802 and 1837 are for a "West Kingdown Farm" and since the rent is 12s 8d and the area is *c.* 56 acres it seems fairly certain this is the West Kingdown Tenement of 1730. The discrepancy in area is likely to be due to the inclusion of *c.* 15 acres of land which would have been common in 1730 but had been enclosed and added to the holding by 1800.

The 1827 deed has a listing of fields most of which can be cross-referenced accurately to the Nempnett Tithe Map, and Figure 75 shows the estimated location of the tenement in 1730, an area of *c.* 41 acres. By 1841 this holding had become known by its present name of Longhouse Farm, which was owned then by Charles Kemeys Kemeys-Tynte Esq.

10. Merry Fields Tenement (Figure 75, top right)

Many detailed records exist for this estate, variously called Merefields, Merefields Hill, and Merry Fields, and which is now known as Merry Hill Farm in Nempnett parish (see DD/S/WH 180 No 7, DD/BRC 17 and DD/RN/43 and 62). At some stage in the late 18th century it appears that land previously on Kingdown Common was added to this estate. Figure 75 shows the estate as it was likely to have been in 1730. Mapped here are the *c.* 43 acres attributed to Merry Hill Farm in the Nempnett Tithe Map, excluding fields previously on the common.

11. Stroud Batch Tenement (Figure 75, lower left)

The best guess for this small tenement is the block of fields in the Regilbury Tithing centred on Upton Farm, Wapsell, Stroud. This allocation has been arrived at largely by a process of elimination, other fields in this area having been associated with other holdings. This map is incomplete, as only *c.* 6 acres are shown compared to *c.* 18 acres in the 1730 survey.

12. Mid Stroud Tenement (Figure 75, lower right)

In the Nempnett Tithe Map there is a block of land of *c.* 41 acres in the Stroud area occupied by Phillip Bennett and owned by John Morgan. Given the location of this holding, the similarity in area, and the fact that in 1730 the tenant was Mary Morgan (with the lives on the tenancy also Morgans), this has been identified as the 1730 Mid Stroud Tenement as shown in Figure 75.

13. Son [Southern] Stroud Tenement (not mapped)

The Regilbury Tithe Map has three fields around and including Wapsell Cottage under separate ownership, and since these fields total *c.* 2.5 acres this is likely to have been the Southern Stroud Tenement. A separate map has not been prepared, but the location is between the southern edge of the Stroud Batch tenement and the north-eastern extent of Mid Stroud Tenement.

14. Church House Tenement, Nempnett (Figure 76, top left)

The distinctive rent of £1 5s 0½d makes it easy to associate this tenement with the deeds DD/S/WH 181 No 23 for two leases in 1756 and 1780 to William Bennett, and to the *c.* 49 acre holding described only as "Lot 26" in the 1811 survey of the "Estates in Regilbury [Manor] in the parish of Nempnett" (DD/FS Box 16/4/1) then also in the tenure of one William Bennett. This 1811 survey has a list of fields most of which can be accurately identified on the Nempnett Tithe Map.

"Lot 26" appears to have been bought by, or passed to, Bengoughs Charity by 1818 and the same listing of fields is given in Bristol Charities (1831, pp 504, 512) together with details of previous leases between the Tyntes and the Bennetts. The 1841 Tithe Map has this holding as owned by Bengoughs Charity, leased to Joseph Bennett and occupied by Martha Keel. Figure 76 shows this Tenement, the mapped area being *c.* 47 acres compared to the 1730 figure of *c.* 52 acres. The main dwelling is Church Farm in Nempnett parish.

15. New House Tenement (Figure 76, top right)

The name "New House Tenement" appears in DD/S/WH 181 No 29 on a deed of 1791 between Lady Tynte and Mary Wooldridge with a rent of 7s and heriot of £1. This deed gives a list of seven fields totalling *c.* 15 acres. In the 1811 survey DD/FS Box 16/4/1 "Lot 39" is noted as "called New House Tenement" and this deed gives a list of five fields totalling *c.* 14 acres and has the same tenant, rent and heriot as the 1791 deed. However, the field names differ between the deeds and it is difficult to cross-reference them to the Tithe Map since they have very similar acreages. Bristol Charities (1831, pp 506, 514) has this tenement as "Lot 39" of the Bengoughs Charity land and in one case has Rees Mogg as the tenant.

The estimate of this tenement mapped in Figure 76 is a block of land of *c.* 14 acres in the Nempnett Tithe Map owned by

Bengoughs Charity, leased to Mary Rees Mogg and occupied by William Stephens. Some of the field names can be confidently matched to one or other of the lists noted above, and given that the Rees Moggs' are descendents of Mary Wooldridge, that the name Rees Mogg appears in the Bristol Charities entry, and the close match in the total area of the holding, this is a fairly confident estimate of the New House Tenement.

This is the first of a series of holdings in the extreme south-east of Nempnett parish, in an area known previously as Pigsty Hole or Pixey Hole. Today there is one residence, Pixey Hall Farm, but in 1841 there were three dwellings. The "New House" was on the north side of the lane, and a building is shown there on the 1888 Ordnance Survey map, about 150m due north of Pixey Hall farm.

16. Roofless Tenement, Now House in Nempnett (Figure 76, lower left)

This tenement can be traced in a similar manner to New House. In 1730 it has a rent of 6s 8d and acreage of *c*. 8 acres. This matches "Lot 28" in the 1811 survey DD/FS Box 16/4/1 where the tenants are Edward Bilbie and John Watts and which has a list of four fields, total area *c*. 7 acres. The mapped area in Figure 76 is the block of land in the Nempnett Tithe Map owned by Bengoughs Charity and occupied by Henry Watts, measuring *c*. 7 acres and also comprising four fields, although there is no evidence of the location of any house associated with this holding.

17. Pigg Stie Hole (Figure 76, lower right)

This tenement does not appear to have passed to the Bengoughs Charity, and is mapped in Figure 76 as the block of land in the Nempnett Tithe Map centred on Pixey Hall Farm, owned and occupied then by Mary Belcher, and totalling *c*. 18 acres. The change of place name from "hole", perhaps originally the Old English *halh* meaning nook, or sunken place, to hall is well documented.[1] The change from Pigg Stie to Pixey is probably less common; it is unfortuante that the history of this particular name seems somewhat unromantic, but it emphases the importance of tracing the history of a name.

18. Pigg Stie Cottage, 40' by 40' (not mapped)

The 1841 Tithe Map has a cottage immediately adjacent to the Pixey Hall farmhouse and this is most likely Pigg Stie Cottage.

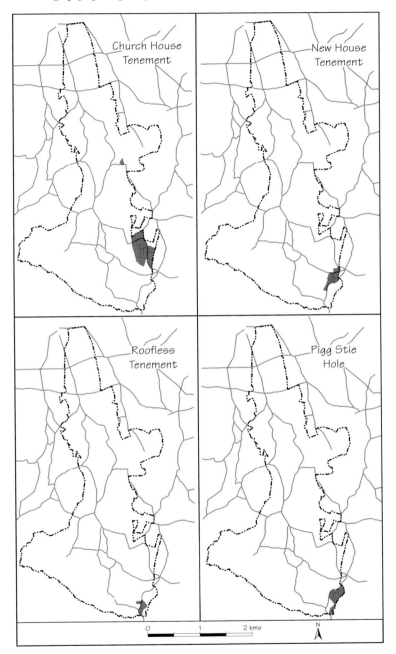

Figure 76: Regilbury Manor 1730: 3 Church House, New House, and Roofless tenements and Pigg Stie Hole

19. East House Tenement (Figure 77, top left)

This is another tenement acquired by Bengoughs Charity in the early 19th century. It is "Lot 27" from the survey of Regilbury in 1811 (DD/FS Box 16/4/1) and in Bristol Charities (1831, pp 504, 512) where a listing of fields is given. Figure 77 shows an estimate of this tenement, based on the "best-fit" between the listing of fields in Bristol Charities and the Nempnett Tithe Map.

The mapped area is *c.* 55 acres, and is centred on East House Farm. This area is somewhat less than the *c.* 66 acres given in the 1730 survey, and there is some uncertainty around West Town, where there are a number of fields called Chickey or Chitty Hill, and on Rugmoor, that was common land until about 1770. East House Tenement is the first of six tenements that in 1730 had rights to common pasture on Rugmoor (as discussed in more detail in Chapter 5). The area shown on Rugmoor is that portion that was allocated to the tenement after enclosure *c.* 1770 using the information provided in documents DD/X/HLL.

20. Home Tenement, Nempnett (Figure 77, top right)

Although there are a large number of deeds that relate to this tenement, it has proved difficult to map with certainty. There is a collection of deeds in DD/S/WH 180 No 16 for the period 1762-1804, which includes a listing of fields and details of how the tenement was split into three around 1774. Parts of this tenement then appear in the 1811 survey DD/FS Box 1/4/1 as "Lots 32, 33 and 37", where they are referred to as being previously part of a "Horts" or "Harts" tenement. The likely explanation here in that this land was occupied by members of the Hort family in the 18th century and the names Home, Hort and Hart have been used interchangeably.

Figure 77 shows the best estimate of this tenement, based on the listing of fields available in the deeds mentioned above. The mapped area is *c.* 67 acres compared to *c.* 79 acres in the 1730 survey. The group of fields in the east of Nempnett parish, just north-west of the church, are clustered around what may be an old farmhouse. Although there is no record of an inhabited building there in the 1841 Tithe Apportionment, the Tithe Map does include a small, unnumbered field that might be a derelict building. The 1888 OS map shows a building here and the pattern of tracks and footpaths which might be indicative of an old farm.

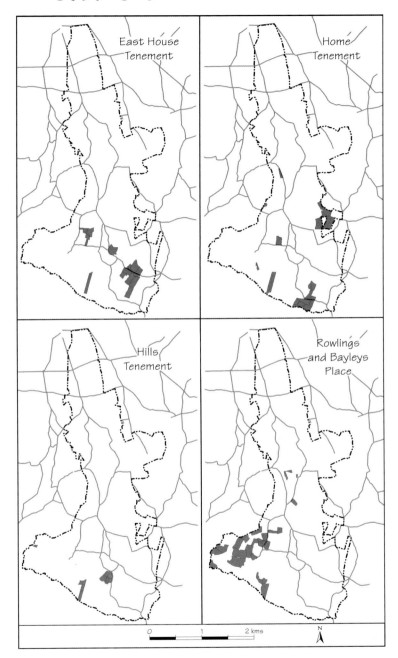

Figure 77: Regilbury Manor 1730: 4: East House, Home and Hills tenements and Rowlings and Bayleys place

21. Hills Tenement, Nempnett (Figure 77, lower left)

This holding is another that passed to Bengoughs Charity, as "Lot 34" in DD/FS Box 16/4/1 and Bristol Charities (1831). These entries can be traced back to the 1730 tenement via deeds covering the period 1740-1791 in DD/S/WH 181 No 17. The mapped area shown in Figure 77 is that owned by Bengoughs Charity, leased to John Stabbins and occupied by Benjamin Weaver in the Nempnett Tithe Map, a total of *c.* 19 acres. This holding is based on a farm located about 175m north-west of Rugmoor Farm which no long exists but is shown on the 1888 OS map and the Tithe Map (see Figure 47 in Chapter 5).

22. Cuckoo's Nest (see Figure 2 in Chapter 1, also Plate 19)

In 1841 there were two properties in central Nempnett at a place known as Cuckoo's Nest, and it seems this holding of a cottage and a small strip of land referred to one of these. Most likely it is the house today known as "Rock House" but it may have been the other smaller cottage that has now disappeared.

23. Rowlings and Bayleys Place (Figure 77, lower right)

This is another holding which passed to Bengoughs Charity and which is well documented in DD/S/WH 180 No 1, DD/FS Box 16/4/1 and Bristol Charities (1831), in the latter two as "Lot 29". The name and the fact that the heriot is two best beasts suggest that this may once have been two holdings. The mapped area shown in Figure 77 is that owned by Bengoughs Charity in the Nempnett Tithe Map, with various tenants and occupiers, matched to the field listings given in the above deeds. The main residence is Old Farm in West Town, and the total area mapped is *c.* 97 acres compared to *c.* 95 given in the 1730 survey.

24. Webbs Tenement (Figure 78, top left)

Only one reference to this tenement has been found; the deeds DD/RN 43 refer to William Sherbourne being the tenant there around 1800. A set of maps dated 1794-1811 of the lands of Isaac Elton Esq. in Nempnett and held by SRO at DD/WY, includes the names of landowners adjacent to Isaac Elton's property and there is one reference to William Sherbourne in the extreme south of the map (see Plate 19). An informed guess, based on the size of this holding, its position in the 1730 survey and the entry on the 1811 Elton map, is that this tenement is associated with Belle Vue Farm, West Town. Figure 78 shows

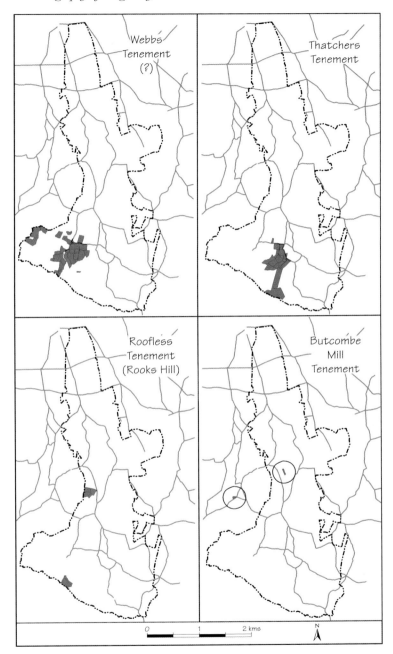

Figure 78: Regilbury Manor 1730: 5 Webbs, Thatchers, Rooks Hill and Butcombe Mill tenements

the location of the *c.* 77 acres of land associated with that farm in the Tithe Map.

25. *Thatcher's Tenement (Figure 78, top right)*

Tracing this tenement has proved difficult. There are a series of references in deeds DD/S/WH 223, 224, 228 and 200 covering the period 1714-1797 which allows a sequence of tenants to be identified (the first being Richard Thatcher) but none of the deeds has a field listing. The last tenant was John Hellier and a tentative assessment has been made that this tenement is Grove Farm, since at the time of the Tithe Map the owner of the land was William Hellier, the amount of land owned by the farm roughly matches that in the 1730 tenement and the farm is in the right part of the parish and includes land on Rugmoor. Further, the 1811 Elton Map (Plate 19) has Grove Farm occupied by one James Hellier. Figure 77 shows this estimate which totals *c.* 62 acres mapped compared to *c.* 58 acres in the 1730 survey.

26. *Roofless Tenement (Rooks Hill) (Figure 78, lower left)*

There are a series of references for the period 1759-1793 in deeds DD/S/WH 180 No 6 that refer to "several fields in Nempnett" and include a listing of five fields. The rent and size suggest these deeds refer to this holding. Two of these fields then appear as "Lot 36" in the 1811 survey (DD/FS Box 16/4/1), where they are described as "part of an estate called Rooks Hill Tenement," and in Bristol Charities (1831, 506, 514).

Figure 78 shows the best estimate of this estate, using the field names given in DD/S/WH 180. The northern part of the holding is in an area where several fields are called Hooks Hill in the Tithe Map. The name Rooks Hill seems more likely to be the correct place-name, given the earlier date of the 1811 deed where this name is used.

27. *Sands Tenement (not mapped)*

There is a reference to this holding in DD/S/WH 181 No 18, where a lease of 1756 between Sir Charles Kemeys Tynte and William Porter is listed as Sands Tenement and refers to "39 acres in Wrington parish and rights on Wrington common", but there is no listing of fields. Given the position of the other holdings discussed so far, and the mention of common land, a likely location for this tenement is on the high land in the north of Wrington parish just to the west of Kingdown Common.

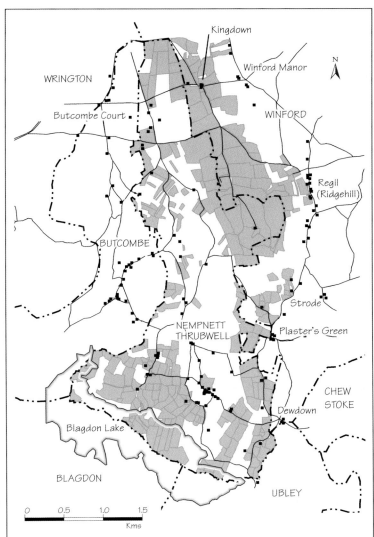

Figure 79: The geography of Regilbury Manor 1730

28. Roofless Tenement (not mapped)

No information on this tenement has been obtained. The fact that it has the same tenant as Sands Tenement and is adjacent in the survey suggests it may too be in Wrington parish, and it has been treated as such in the later analysis.

29. Wades Roofless Tenement (not mapped)

This is the only tenement for which no information has been

Parish	acres	%
Nempnett Thrubwell	779.4	65.5
Winford – previously Regilbury Tithing	333.7	28.1
Winford – previously Nempnett	28.0	2.3
Wrington	42.2	3.5
Butcombe	6.1	0.5
Totals	1189.4	100

Table 3: Analysis of holdings of Regilbury Manor in 1730 by parish

found and no estimate has been made as to its location.

30. Butcombe Mill Tenement (Figure 78, lower right)
The deeds DD/S/WH 181 No 25 trace the history of the Butcombe Mill Tenement over the period 1663-1794, when the holding comprised of two pieces of land, the Mill and Swithy or Swilly Mead, as shown in Figure 78. By 1900 Butcombe Mill had been transferred to Butcombe parish, and later records refer only to Swithy/Swilly Mead, for example "Lot 38" in DD/FS Box 16/4/1 and Bristol Charities (1831).

SUMMARY AND CONCLUSIONS

The previous sections have outlined, holding-by-holding, the process by which the geography of Regilbury Manor in 1730 was reconstructed. The final outcome is shown in Figure 79, which shows the likely geography of the manor's lands in 1730 in relation to current day settlement. As well as the individual holdings previously discussed this map also shows land at the north of Nempnett parish which was common in 1730 but which appears to have been under the control of Regilbury Manor (as evidenced in the ownership given in the 1841 Tithe Apportionment). The two holdings totalling 42 acres which were identified as being within Wrington parish, but whose location is not known, have not been mapped, nor has the Broadway Down holding of 5.5 acres in Butcombe. It seems likely that the location of the majority of these three holdings is on the high ground of Broadfield Down adjacent to Kingdown Common.

The total area mapped in Figure 79 is 1141 acres, equivalent to 92.8% of the 1730 survey of 1230 acres. The degree of confidence that can be placed in the accuracy of this map depends upon an assessment of the holding-by-holding reconstruction discussed in the previous sections. Generally it appears that holdings changed relatively little between 1730 and 1841, and the large number of deeds from the Manor together with the information in the Bristol Charities report means that most holdings appear to have been identified with a large degree of certainty. It seems very unlikely that the general pattern shown in Figure 79 is misleading.

Table 3 shows an analysis of the Manor of Regilbury's land in 1730 by parish, using the boundaries of 1841 and 1900, where a total of 1189 acres, 96.7% of the 1730 holdings, has been confidently allocated to parishes. Using the 1841 boundaries the majority of the Manor's land, 807 acres (67.9%) lay within the parish of Nempnett Thrubwell, with the major part of the remainder, 334 acres (28.1%), in Regilbury Tithing of Blagdon parish, with small amounts of land in Wrington (*c.* 42 acres or 3.5%) and Butcombe (*c.* 6 acres or 0.5%).

Using the 1900 boundaries as the basis for analysis, just over 779 acres (65.5%) of the Manor's land is within Nempnett Thrubwell, *c.* 362 acres (30.4%) lies within what is now Winford parish (all of this land was previously within Regilbury Tithing or Nempnett parish), and the same small amounts of land are in Wrington and Butcombe.

The analysis presented here has shown, for the first time I believe, the degree to which the Manor of Regilbury was important in the affairs of the parish of Nempnett Thrubwell. It seems that about half the area of the parish in 1730 was under the control of Regilbury, making the Manor a key player in the destiny of parish. Much remains to be discovered, for example the degree to which the Manor's holdings changed over time, and what other manors held land in the parish. The next chapter addresses the latter question.

9   Other Manors

INTRODUCTION

In this chapter the focus is on manors other than Regilbury that are known to have had holdings in the parish of Nempnett Thrubwell. The evidence about these "other manors" is much more fragmentary than that available for Regilbury and the overall pattern of manorial ownership in the parish is complex. Francis Neale, an expert on the manorial history of Butcombe, summarises the situation as "a confusing and occasionally conflicting series of genealogies and property transfers" involving manors owning land in Butcombe, Nempnett, and other nearby parishes. The aim of this chapter is to draw together and summarise what is known about the manors that had land holdings in the parish of Nempnett Thrubwell over the period 1100-1900.

An overview of which manors appear to have held land in Nempnett Thrubwell, and the length of time over which information is available for each manor, is shown in Figure 80. There is information on Regilbury Manor throughout the period from the Domesday Book in 1086 to the 20th century, although for certain periods this information is very sparse, but for the "other manors" information is generally available for shorter time periods.

There are many references to Thrubwell Manor in the 13th century, when it was in control of the Bretasche family. Around 1315 this manor became joined by marriage with the Manor of Butcombe held by the Perceval family, and information on this Butcombe Manor can be traced from the Domesday Book through to the end of the 17th century. A second manor in Butcombe is also believed to have held land in Nempnett; this second manor was probably owned originally by St. John's Hospital in Bristol and later by the Lords of the Manor at Butcombe Court.

There a few scattered references in the 14th and early 15th century to John of Clevedon holding land in Thrubwell, and it appears that this land then passed to the two Manors in Butcombe just discussed. Documents of the 18th century refer to "the Manor of Compton Magna and Badgworth &c" holding land in Nempnett. Finally, there is the mysterious Beechen Stoke Manor, said by Collinson in 1791 to lie "on the confines of this parish [Nempnett] and that of Chew Stoke" but whose location is now unknown.

THRUBWELL MANOR

There are a series of references to the Bretasche Family, also spelt Britashe, owning and occupying the Manor of Thrubwell from the late 12th century to the early 14th century.[1] The family are said by some to have proceeded originally from a younger branch of the ancient Counts of Guisnes in Flanders, but Collinson says they probably derived their appellation from a small manor in the parish of Street near Glastonbury called Brutesayshe, where once they had the chief of their possessions.

Collinson describes the arms of Bretasche as, Sable, a lion rampant argent, double queued, crowned or – that is to say an upright silver lion with two tails and a gold crown, on a black background; a lion is said to symbolise deathless courage, the silver colour (argent) peace and sincerity, and black (sable) constancy and sometimes grief.[2] A reconstruction of what the coat of arms might have looked like is shown in Figure 81.

The first dated reference to an individual member of this family is in 1177-8, when "Richard de Bretasche, Lord of the Manor, was fined ten marks [£6.70] for trespassing in the king's adjacent forest of Cheddar, or Winford".[3] Richard is known to have died in 1198 and to have been succeeded by his son John, who married Margaret, widow of Warin de Ralege, and daughter of Lord Boteler of Overley.

In 1201 a there was a court case concerning a dispute over land thought to have been held by Richard Bretasche, which is recorded in Somerset Pleas: Rolls of the Itinerant Justices also referred to as The Assize Rolls. The full text is as follows:

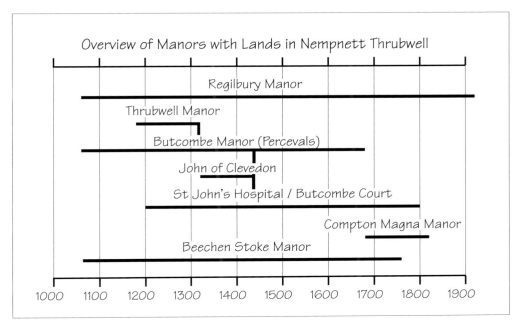

Figure 80: Overview of Manors with holdings in Nempnett Thrubwell

The assize comes to recognise whether Richard Bretasche, father of John, was seised in his demesne as of fee of twelve acres of wood, with the appurtenances, in Trubewel' on the day he died, etc., and whether the same John be his heir, which land Elyas son of William holds. The jury say that Richard died so seised. Judgment: let John have his seisin, and Elyas is in mercy for unjust detention. And be it known that this assize was taken in the absence of Elyas through his default.[4]

Summarised in simple, modern-day English, the case concerns 12 acres of wood in Thrubwell. The jury at the assize is asked "did Richard Bretasche own it at his death and does his son John now own it?" The jury answers "Yes" to both these questions and says that Elyas son of William, who claims it and holds it, has no right to do so. This case is of interest in its own right, and it is also one of the earliest references to the place-name Thrubwell.

In 1238-9 there is a second dispute, recorded in the Feet of Fines for the County of Somerset, involving John Bretasche, which throws further light onto early landowners in Thrubwell. The full entry is:

> At St. Bride's, London, in three weeks of Easter; between John Bretasche, querent; and Brother Roger, Master of the Hospital of St. John of Radeclive, deforciant; for common of pasture in Trubewelle, namely, in the wood called Hugrave. John quit claimed all rights; for this the Master conceded to John a virgate of land in Trubewelle which Walter son of Norman held; to hold of the said Master, together with half a virgate which he already held in the same vill the gift of Elyas son of William; rendering annually ten shillings and six pence [52p] for all service save regal service. And if John or his heirs default in payment, the Master may distrain until full payment is made.[5]

In layman's terms this records that John Bretasche granted rights of common pasture in Hugrave Wood to Brother Roger, Master of St. John's Hospital, Redcliffe, Bristol, in exchange for a virgate of land (in very rough terms about 60 acres) in Thrubwell. John already held half a virgate of land from Brother Roger which was a gift from Elyas son of William, so now John holds 1½ virgates for which he pays 10s 6d [52p] rent in lieu of all services due to Roger, with the exception of services due to the King. The reference establishes that both John Bretasche and St. John's Hospital, Bristol, owned land in Thrubwell at this time. The place-name Hugrave is likely to be an early spelling of Howgrove.

An agreement between John Bretasche and the rector of Compton Martin regarding the building of a chapel at Thrubwell dated 1242 is recorded in the Calendar of the Manuscripts of the Dean and Chapter of Wells. The full reference is:

> Indenture of agreement made 1242, between Sir Robert Rector of Cumptone [Compton Martin] and Sir John Bretasche the elder, whereby the rector licences a chapel erected by the said Sir John in his court of Trubbewell [Thrubwell], upon condition that such chapel be subject to the mother church of Compton, that the chaplain shall be presented to the rector and by him to the archdeacon of Bath to be admitted, and in their presence shall swear fealty to the rector and to save him harmless so far as in him lies, that the lords and ladies of the said place with their

Figure 81: Recreation of Bretasche coat of arms

household shall in due course three times a year on the principal feasts visit the church of Empnete [Nempnett], which is a chapel of the mother church of Compton, if they be dwelling there; that then they shall have licence to hear divine service in their said chapel, provided the chaplain pay to the parson all obventions therein. Assent of J Bishop of Bath, Master H Tesson archdeacon of Bath, Nicholas patron of the said church, and R the rector aforesaid.[6]

This is an important reference as it establishes that Thrubwell Manor must have been of sufficient status to merit the erection of its own chapel, and it also indicates that the Manor must have been within the jurisdiction of Nempnett Church. Unfortunately there are no further records of exactly where this chapel was located, but the most likely spot seems to be somewhere in the vicinity of Thrubwell Farm.

Collinson has a number of other references to this John Bretasche. In 1219 he is found entering into a composition with Adam Gianne and Anne his wife, concerning certain lands in Crewkerne, part of the dowry of the said Margaret from her former husband. In 1242 he is recorded for non-appearance before the justices' itinerant, in the hundreds of Chew, Wedlow, Portbury, Hareclive, and Chewton, in all which hundreds he possessed estates. Not long after this he occurs as a witness to a deed of Geoffrey de Craucombe, whereby he granted his Manor of Craucombe in this county to the church of the Blessed Virgin Mary of Studley in the county of Oxford.

John died in 1245 and was succeeded by his son, also called John. Collinson describes this second John as "Lord of the Manor of Thrubwell, which he held of Gilbert de Clare, Earl of

Gloucester, by the service of half a knight's fee [at which time] The profits of the court, were valued at two shillings [10p]." In 1258 he presented William de Sodden to William Briton, chief justice of the forest, to be his woodward of the forest of Winford, who was admitted accordingly. In 1260 he married Engeretta and in 1263 he joined with his wife in a grant to William Bozun and his heirs of one messuage and three furlongs of arable land in Heathfield in this county, as also two furlongs and a tenement in Ford; reserving an acknowledgment of two barbed arrows, or in lieu thereof one penny, to be paid annually at Easter.

The elder John died in 1287, and his only child Joan inherited his estate, and she at around this time married Roger Lord Perceval of Butcombe, so that Thrubwell Manor was united with this Manor of Butcombe. Two deeds from this period with Joan's seal survive at the Bristol Record Office.[7] The first dated 1314, which is shown in Figure 82, reads:

> Johanna, relict of Sir Roger Perceval, daughter and heiress of Sir John de Brutasche [Bretasche] grants to the master, brethren and sisters of the Hospital of St. John the Baptist of La Redecleue [Redcliffe] of Bristol and their successors other rights in two crofts lying in Blakedone [Blagdon] and Budicome [Butcombe] of which one is called Dunggecrofte and the other le Worthey. Seal of Johanna, Dated at Thrubewelle Tuesday in the feast of St Barnabas the Apostle [11 June] 7 Edward II [1314]. Witnesses: Peter de Rillebury, John Sprot, John de Sheptone, Robert de Feghelonde [Failand], Robert de Rillebury, and many others.

The deed confirms the lineage of Joan, as the heiress of Sir John Bretasche and then the wife of Sir Roger Perceval, and shows she was resident still at Thrubwell, presumably at the Manor. The deed identifies again the Hospital of St. John as having land interests in the local area. The witnesses Peter and Robert de Rillebury are likely to have been residents at Regilbury at this time (see Chapter 6 above).

The second deed reads:

> Joan, relict of Sir Roger Perceval, daughter and heiress of Sir John de Bretasche, quitclaims to the master of the hospital of St. John the Baptist of la Redecleue

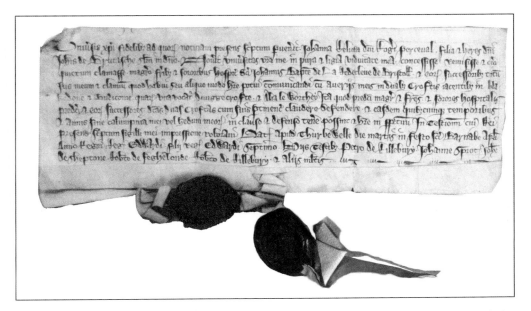

Figure 82: Deed of 1315 between Joan Perceval (nee Bretasche) and the Hospital of St John the Baptist, Redcliffe, Bristol

[Redcliffe] at Bristoll, the brethren and sisters, her right in 11½ acres of [arable] land in Thrubewelle and Budicome [Butcombe] and in that meadow called Wateleymede in Budicome, whereof 9 acres of land and 1 perch lie near the house late of Grecia le Seriaunt and stretches to the King's Highway towards Bristoll, and 2 acres and 1 perch lie in five pieces in Budicome in the field called Redefeld; which land a certain Stephen, master of the aforesaid hospital, had by gift and grant of the said Sir Roger, formerly her lord and husband, other inheritance, in exchange for 11½ acres of land in Stapelfelde; and the meadow lies in Budicome in a meadow called Wateleymede, which meadow Sir Roger held and granted to Peter de Rillebury in exchange for 3 perches of land in Budicome lying in a field called Garstone under Bikenhulle. Seal of Joan. Dated Thurbewelle Tuesday in the feast of St Barnabas [11 June] I Edward II. Witnesses: Peter of Rillebury, John Sprot, John of Sheptone, Robert of Feghelonde, Robert of Rillebury and many others.

This deed is similar to the first, but is noteworthy in addition for confirming the Hospital of St. John as owning lands in Thrubwell and for the mention of Bikenhulle, literally "Beacon Hill", which appears to be an early reference to the place-name Bicknell.

The marriage between Joan Bretasche and Lord Roger Perceval meant that Thrubwell Manor became part of Butcombe Manor. At the time of Domesday Butcombe Manor was owed by the Bishop of Coutances and held by Fulcan, and was taxed at three hides. It then passed to one of the name Bodicombe, of whom Walter and Roger possessed it before 1113, after which date it passed to the de Mohun family. In 1200 it was given to Sir Richard Perceval when he married the daughter of William de Mohun. It then stayed in the male Perceval line until the time of King William III (1689-1702) when it fell to Anne Perceval, who married first Evan Lloyd of Shropshire, and second Thomas Salisbury of Flintshire, and divided the estate and sold it to various persons unknown.[8]

There are only a very few known references to Percevals holding land in Thrubwell over the period 1315-1700. One appears in the English manuscript collection at Vascar College, Ploughkeepsie, New York, where there is a note of an abstract of the Court Roll of 3 January 1654 that refers to Richard Perceval as Lord of the Manor of Thrubwell, Butcombe, and Stoke Bishop.[9] A second reference dated between 1544 and 1551 is of a dispute between William Vowles and Edmund Perceval over a house called "Percyvalles Place" and lands in Thrubwell and Butcombe, that also includes a reference to Perceval having "several .. Thrubwell tenants".[10]

The ownership of Thrubwell Manor can therefore be traced with some certainty from the time of the Bretasche family in the late 12th century, to its disposal as part of the Percevals' Butcombe Estate around 1700. However, there are few if any details from this period as to its exact location. Rutter refers to Thrubwell Manor House being an old residence which "was nearly destroyed during the great rebellion," presumably a reference to the civil war. Its location is described as being on the borders of Broadfield Down and attached to Butcombe Court. Collinson says the Manor was in both Butcombe and Nempnett Parish, and that its name is derived from a spring rising in Nempnett.[11]

These brief descriptions of Thrubwell Manor, plus contemporary place-name evidence, suggest Thrubwell Farm was the location for the Manor, a view shared by Frances Neale.[12]

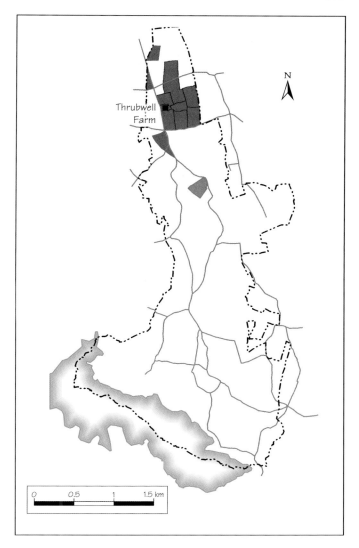

Figure 83: Lands of Thrubwell Farm 1841

Supporting evidence that Thrubwell Farm may well be the site of Thrubwell Manor comes from a 1786 Court case Somers v James,[13] that concerns an argument over the marriage settlement between Mary Jones and John Somers made in 1737, after John Somers died intestate in 1787, Mary having died before.

In 1754 John Somers and his wife Mary had bought an estate described as:

"all that Manor or Lordship or reputed Manor or Lordship of Batcombe, otherwise Butcombe Thrubwell, with the appurtenances in the said County of Somerset together with several closes and parcels of land therein particularly mentioned situate in the several parishes of Butcombe and Nempnett Blagdon, Over Weare and Henbury in the several counties of Gloucestershire and Somerset".

Elsewhere the description used refers to

"the said Manor or Lordship or reputed Manor or Lordship of Batcombe, otherwise Butcombe Thrubwell, messuages, tenements, closes, pieces and parcels or ground, land and hereditaments and all other premises therein mentioned to be situate, lying and being in the several parishes and places of Butcombe, Nempnett, Blagdon, Thrubwell and Henbury".

This reference to a Lordship of "Butcombe Thrubwell" strongly suggests there is some relation between this estate and the old Thrubwell Manor. The lands in Over Weare and Henbury were sold before 1787, and the main dispute concerns a farm holding in Nempnett, by then in the ownership of George James. This holding is noted as being roughly 96 acres and there is a list of field names, that, when cross-referenced to the Tithe Map, clearly identify this holding as Thrubwell Farm. At the time of the Tithe Map (1841) George James was still the owner of Thrubwell Farm, with a total of 93 acres in Nempnett and a small acreage in Butcombe. It is also of interest to note that Donne's 1742 Map of Somerset has the name Mr. Sommers close to Thrubwell Farm (see Figure 40 in Chapter 4).

The land of Thrubwell Farm as recorded in the Tithe Map is shown in Figure 83. It seems extremely likely that this mapped area bears some relationship to the old Thrubwell Manor.

ST. JOHN'S HOSPITAL / BUTCOMBE COURT / BROADWELL DOWN

There are a small number of references over the period 1200-1500 to The Hospital of St. John the Baptist, in Redcliffe, Bristol, owning land in Thrubwell and Butcombe. In 1239 there was an exchange of rights and land in Thrubwell between St. John's and John Bretasche of Thrubwell Manor, and in 1314 an agreement

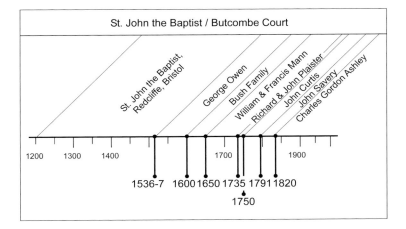

St. John the Baptist / Butcombe Court

St. John the Baptist, Redcliffe, Bristol

George Owen
Bush Family
William & Francis Mann
Richard & John Plaister
John Curtis
John Savery
Charles Gordon Ashley

1200   1300   1400   1700   1900

1536-7 1600 1650 1735 1791 1820
              1750

Figure 84: Timeline of the ownership of Butcombe Court

between St. John's and Joan Bretasche-Perceval, as discussed in the previous section.

The Hospital, which was a religious house rather than a centre for medicine, is believed to have been founded around 1200 by John Farcey or Farceyn, and appears to have been close to St. Mary Redcliffe, since a deed of the time of King John (1199-1216) stipulates that a hospital should have its water supplied from a well at St. Mary Redcliffe. Although relatively little is known about the hospital, it acquired, presumably through donations, a series of land holdings in Butcombe and Thrubwell, a manor house in Butcombe, and the advowson (the right to appoint the clergyman) of St. Michael's the parish church of Butcombe.[14]

According to Collinson, after the dissolution (1536-7) the Hospital was granted to George Owen, the King's physician, together with the manor, rectory, and advowson of the church of Butcombe. These then passed to the Bush family. A possible reference to the Bush family is to be found in a deed at the Public Records Office (ref. C147/154) which includes a "John Busshe of Brodwellsdowne in Butcombe". If this is the same family it suggests that at this time the manor might have been called Broadwell Down or similar and may be the manor shown on Saxton's 1575 Map of Somerset (see Figure 64 and chapter 7).

The widow of John Bush then married William Mann of London, so the Manns became Lords of the Manor, until William's grandson Francis sold the same on 29 September 1735 to Richard Plaister. John Plaister, Richard's son, then conveyed it to John Curtis, whose son sold it to John Savery the owner in Collinson's time. The name Mr. Curtis appears at Butcombe

Court on Donne's 1742 map of Somerset (Figure 40), which is consistent with this account. This time-line of the ownership of Butcombe Court is summarised in Figure 84, although some of the dates used are approximate.

From the ownership line it appears that the site of this Manor is Butcombe Court (and that Butcombe Court was separate from the Butcombe Manor owned by the Percevals as described in the previous section). Thus at the time of the Tithe Map the owner was Charles Gordon Ashley, and when Butcombe Court was sold on Thursday 8 April 1948 a newspaper report of the sale says: "George Bendall is now Lord of the Manor of Butcombe. [as] the title goes with Butcombe Court".[15]

There are no known documents relating to the St. John's/ Butcombe Court Manor which describe the location of the lands in Thrubwell. However, there are two examples of references that might be relevant here. First, within certain deeds of Regilbury Manor there are several references to land "late of Mr. Man [also spelt Mann]." Typically these occur in the descriptions of individual parcels of land, when the owners of adjacent pieces of land are identified. For example, in a deed of 1811 Footbury Close is described a "close of three acres having... on the north and west land of one Mr. Man". Careful cross-checking of these named fields to the Tithe Map suggests that all lands once owned by Mr. Man or Mann were in 1841 owned by John Anderson and were part of Howgrove Farm.[16]

This analysis suggests that a reasonable working hypothesis is that Howgrove Farm and perhaps Bicknell Farm were once linked with this manor – see Figure 85. Further supporting "evidence" includes: (a) the use of the place-names Howgrove and Bicknell in the early documents concerning the land owned by St. John's Hospital, (b) both farms are in the north-west part of the parish adjacent to Butcombe, which appears to be the general area to which the parish- or tithing-name Thrubwell applied, (c) there is a long history of settlement at Bicknell Farm, including evidence of Iron Age settlement and a 13th century windmill, (d) at the time of the Tithe Map a number of pieces of land around Bicknell Farm were owned by Howgrove Farm, suggesting the two places might have been linked in the past, and (e) there is no evidence to link either of these farms to Regilbury Manor.

A second reference to Francis Mann appears in the documents relating to the enclosure of Rugmoor in the south of the parish, which until *c.* 1778 was common land.[17] One of the documents

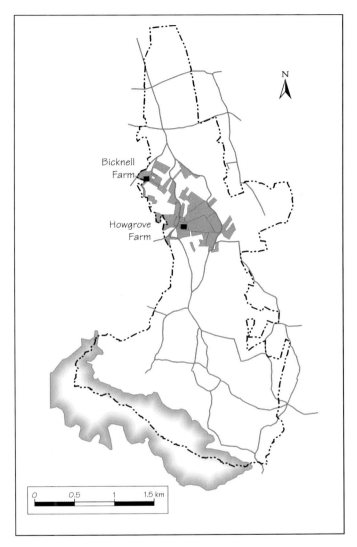

Figure 85: Lands of Bicknell and Howgrove Farms 1841

relating to the enclosure of the common is an examination of Mary Holbrook, a local resident, who describes Mr. Mann as "one of the two Lords of the Fee" of the common in *c.* 1710. Other documents relate that the lands at the eastern end of the common, in 1778 owned by Samuel Sage, Henry Hellier, Christopher Young, and John Cam, were previously owned by Francis Mann Esq. This is consistent with the time-line of the St. John's/Butcombe Court Estate which has Francis Mann selling the estate in 1735. (See Chapter 5 for more details of the enclosure of Rugmoor.)

These documents suggest that there were four farms previously owned by Francis Mann that had rights to common land on Rugmoor. Based on the analysis of the holdings of Regilbury Manor discussed in the previous chapter, and the local geography, a working hypothesis is that these farms were Rugmoor Farm, Street Farm, Londs Farm (now Highlands) and Greenhouse Farm (now Mary Paddock). The holdings of these farms as recorded by the Tithe Map of 1841 are shown in Figure 86. The contiguous nature of the holdings shown in Figure 86 gives some credence to the theory that they have a common history, but whether this area was indeed once a part of the St. John's/Butcombe Court Manor, or has a different history, perhaps having once been part of Regilbury Manor and then having been sold to Francis Mann, is a question that requires further research.

SIR JOHN OF CLEVEDON

There are few scattered references to the Clevedon family owning lands in Thrubwell in the period 1315-1428. A surviving deed of 1315 records the grant of the Manors of Throbwelle, Budicombe and Stoke to Sir John of Clevedon, his wife Emma and his sons John and Matthew, from Reginald de Campo Arnulfi.[18] Little is known of this deed. Reginald de Campo Arnulfi may have been Reginald Chapernowne of Ilfracombe, who lived 1272-1333, and was Lord of Tywardreath.

In 1316 there is the entry in Feudal Aids for "Budencombe, Johannes de Clyvedon." In 1346 in the Nomina Villarium the entry for "Raggel [Regilbury]" is Johannes de Clyvedon and Petrus de Rillebury. A second entry for 1346 in Feudal Aids says Mathew de Clyvedon holds half a knight's fee in "Bodycomb [Butcombe]" previously held by Roger Perceval. Finally, there is an entry of 1428 in Feudal Aids that says half a knight's fee is held in "Bidecombe [Butcombe]" by Richard Perceval and the Master of St. John's Bristol that used to be held by Mathew of Clyvedon.[19]

From these references it appears that the Clevedon family briefly held land in Butcombe and Thrubwell, possibly land previously held by the Percevals, but that by 1428 this land was under the control of the two Butcombe Manors owned by the Percevals and St. John's Hospital. In her work on Butcombe Francis Neale mentions Manors "changing, joining or subdividing

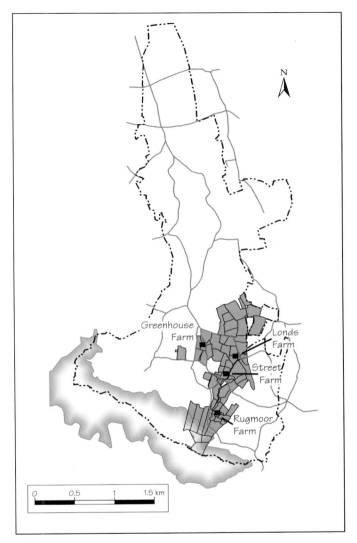

Figure 86: Lands of Greenhouse, Londs, Street and Rugmoor Farms 1841

as the local families intermarried, died out or sold lands" and this may be such an example.

COMPTON MAGNA MANOR

Mention of this Manor owning land in Nempnett is contained in the will of William Prowse (1590-1670) of West Street, Axbridge within the parish of Compton Bishop. In his will there is described his ownership of:

the manour of Compton Magna and Badgworth &c. in the said County of Somersett situate, lying, and being within the parishes of Compton Bishop, Badgworth, Wedmore, Weare, Biddesham, Allerton Morte (Mark), South Brent, Lympsham, Weston Super Mare, Winscombe, Banwell, Congresbury, Weeke St. Lawrence, Portishead, **Nempnett**, Well (Wells), Wookey, Claston, Spaxton, Cannington, Otterhampton, Stogursey, Stockline, Lovell and Fiddington in the said county of Somersett.[20]

It appears that this land passed by his will to his cousin's son John Prowse of Compton House, Axbridge and Compton Bishop, who died in 1688, then to his son John Prowse of Compton Bishop, who died in 1710, then to his son Thomas Prowse of Compton Bishop, who died in 1767, and then to his coheiress and daughter Elizabeth Prowse (1749-1826).

In 1770 within the Copy Act concerning the Estates of Thomas Prowse, Lot 1 to be passed to Elizabeth Prowse includes Nympnet Farm, with acreage of 114-3-1 (acres, rods and perches), then in the occupation of one Samuel Vowles, and Ashils Wood, acreage 9-0-1.[21] Elizabeth Prowse married John Mordaunt (1734-1806) in 1769 and Sir Charles Kemeys Tynte was a trustee of the marriage settlement. So it appears that the component of the Manor of Compton Magna within Nempnett parish was Nempnett Farm.

On the maps of Nempnett Thrubwell showing Isaac Elton's land, which date to *c.* 1810 (Plate 19), Lady Prowse's name occurs several times in locations consistent with her owning Nempnett Farm, with the farmhouse apparently in the occupation of Samuel Peach Esq.[22] In the 1841 Tithe Map Nempnett Farm is owned and occupied by one John Wilton.

These details strongly suggest that Nempnett Farm was from some time before 1670 part of the Compton Magna Manor owned by the Prowse family, and continued to be owned by them until some time between 1810 and 1841. The lands of Nempnett Farm in 1841 are shown in Figure 87.

BEECHEN STOKE MANOR

This Manor is the most mysterious of those associated with Nempnett. It is spelt in many ways, including Beechen Stoke,

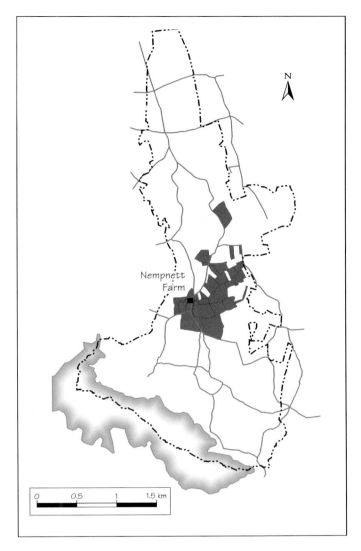

Figure 87: Lands of Nempnett Farm 1841

Beauchamp Stoke, and Birchin Stoke, and in other similar ways. Collinson says it is "situate on the confines of Nempnett and Chew Stoke parishes," and the Rev Eyton in his analysis of the Somerset Domesday Book says it is an "adjunct" of Nempnett Thrubwell.[23] But later authors have been unable to trace its location, and the more recent analysis of Somerset Domesday by Thorne and Thorne refer to it as "lost." [24] However, given the possible links with Nempnett it is worth summarising what is known about this manor.

Beechen Stoke is thought to have been recorded in the Domesday Book. Stuart Morland's detailed analysis of Somerset Domesday[25] suggests that there are two entries, both half-hide estates owned by Serlo de Burci:

> Serlo holds [Beechen] Stoke himself. Everwacer held it before 1066; it paid tax for half a hide. Land for one plough; with one slave it is there in lordship. Meadow 1½ acres; woodland 4 furlongs wide and 1 furlong wide. 13 cattle; 12 pigs; 27 sheep; 20 goats. Value 10s.

> [Beechen] Stoke has been added to this [Chillyhill Manor, Chew Stoke]. Aelfric held it as a manor before 1066; it paid tax for ½ hide. Land for 1 plough, which is there with 2 smallholders and 1 villager. Meadow 1½ acres. Value 10s; when Serlo acquired it 20s.

Collinson says the name is derived "from the family of Beauchamp, or de Bello Campo, who once possessed it," adding that it has always been "held of the honour of Gloucester", that is that any knights' fees would be due to Gloucester. The earliest dated reference in Collinson is "in the time of Edward I [1272-1307] Robert de Walton and his heirs held the tenth part of one knight's fee here."

In 1299 there is an entry in Feet of Fines for a dispute that appears relevant:

> At York in the morrow of St. John Baptist; between William de Burne, clerk, querent; and Amicia daughter of John de Barry of Bychenestok, deforciant; for a messuage and a virgate of land in Bodicombe and Threbwell. Plea of covenant was summoned. Amicia acknowledged the right of William, to hold of the Chief Lords of the Fee; and she warranted against all men: for this William gave Amicia thirty marcs [£20].[26]

Bychenestok is one of the many spellings of Beechen Stoke, so this reference suggests Amicia of Beechen Stoke had an interest in land in Thrubwell [Threwell].

In 1326 Collinson says William Martin, descendant of Serlo de Burci, held a fourth part of a knight's fee in "Bychenestok", which was previously held by Peter de Sancta Cruce. The Sancta

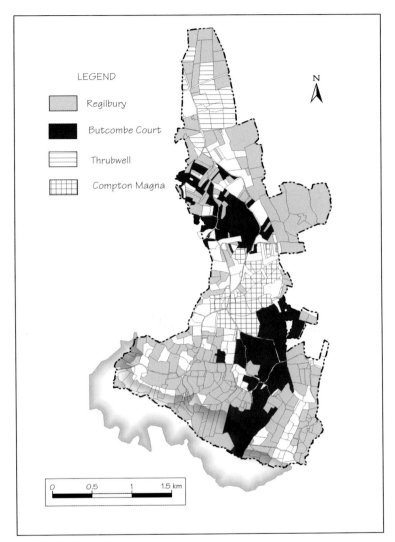

Figure 88:
Reconstruction of the
possible geography
of the Manors of
Nempnett Thrubwell

LEGEND

Regilbury

Butcombe Court

Thrubwell

Compton Magna

N

0   0.5   1   1.5 km

Cruce family had interests in Compton Martin and Roberto de Santa Cruce appears as a witness to several grants concerning land in or near Nempnett in the Cartulary of Flaxley Abbey thought to date to *c.* 1200.[27]

Collinson says further that in 1350 "the heir of John de Leycester held the tenth part, and Phillip de Walleis the fourth part of a [knight's] fee in Birchenstoke", and that in 1513 "an inquisition taken at Wells 23 October 4 Henry VIII it was found that Thomas Ive died seized of the manor of Bechenstok, and that he held the same as of honour of Gloucester". Finally Collinson says "Mr. Page, now or late of Bristol, is the present lord".

Despite this timeline presented by Collinson, whose work is held in very high esteem by historians, later authors have been unable to determine the location of Beechen Stoke, and it remains an unresolved puzzle in the local history of this area. A possibility which might warrant further research is that the Manor might be linked to the deserted hamlet of Long Thorn.

CONCLUSION

The manorial history of Nempnett Thrubwell parish is complex. This chapter has attempted to draw together for the first time the many references to manors other than Regilbury which appear to have had holdings in the parish. Doubtless this list in incomplete, but it is at least a start.

A number of different manors have held land in the parish, although exactly how many is not clear. Some references are very fragmentary so that tracing complete lines of ownership is very difficult if not impossible, and much uncertainty remains. Because most of these references are early ones there is also very little direct evidence of what parts of the parish came under the ownership of these other manors. However, a start has been made here on trying to recreate the geography of these manors, and an estimated map of manorial holdings in *c.* 1700 is shown in Figure 88.

There is a great deal of uncertainty about Figure 88, and it is presented as a provisional estimate that might form the starting point for further research, rather than as a finished piece of work.

10   An Overview

This final chapter presents a selective overview and summary of the history of the parish of Nempnett Thrubwell from its earliest days through to roughly 1850, with the focus mainly on the landscape of the parish, its fields and pattern of settlement. It draws together some themes discussed in previous chapters and tries to answer some questions which have been raised. It does so in a way that is an interpretation, that is to say it is speculative, but the speculations are based on a mixture of empirical evidence and current archaeological thinking.[1]

The earliest visitors to Nempnett probably came here some 6,000-10,000 years ago. They were hunter-gatherers of the early Stone Age, whose main preoccupation in life would have been getting enough to eat. The forests which dominated the area then would have provided hunting grounds for deer, smaller mammals and birds, as well as hazel nuts and other fruits and vegetables. The river and the marshy land around would also have provided much food in the way of birds, and their eggs, and fish. The people of that age were largely nomadic, but there may have already been developing a sense of ownership, that this part of the countryside "belonged" to a particular group, who spent most of their time here, finding it provided sufficient food and resources to support them.

By around 4,000BC, perhaps later, Neolithic peoples had learned to cultivate the land, to clear land for crops and domestic animals, although probably their clearings were used for only a few years until the land became infertile, when they would have moved on to clear new areas. Although the struggle for survival would still have been difficult, populations increased and areas were marked out as belonging to a particular group. People now had enough time to build monuments to their gods and ancestors. We know there were people here in Nempnett at this time because they built Fairy's Toot, probably both as a marker of their territory and as a local focus of ritual activity. For larger parties or ceremonies the local people would have gone to Stanton Drew, to the huge stone circles there, to celebrate important festivals and to meet with local neighbours and exchange gifts, commodities and news.

Fairy's Toot may have marked the western extent of the local Nempnett people, and they may also have built a ceremonial site on the eastern edge of their territory, on a spot with a fine view and an imposing approach, so that outsiders approaching from the east would have seen it – the place where now stands the parish church St. Mary's. Probably there was a marker on the northern edge of their land up on Felton Common while the river (Yeo) marked the southern edge. The parish of Nempnett Thrubwell, though not of that name, was already in existence, a unit of land providing a group of Stone Age people with land for their crops and animals, wood for their fires and houses, and stone for their tools and monuments.

The period from about 2,000BC to 43AD, the Bronze and Iron Ages, would have seen the people become increasingly sophisticated, using first bronze and then iron. By the end of this period fields would have become permanent, their fertility being maintained by natural animal fertilisers, and some of the fields laid out at this time may still be with us today. The people of this age built more barrows to mark the edge of their territory, and to commemorate their dead, and some of these are also still intact today. Probably the locals took over and continued to use the ceremonial sites of their predecessors - the "holy" sites on the western edge of their land at Fairy's Toot, and on the eastern edge at the church. In the Iron Age the lord and selected companions would have travelled to the nearby "Forts" at Maes Knoll, Burledge (overlooking the south-east corner of Chew Valley Lake), Burrington, Dolebury and Congresbury for regional gatherings and ceremonies.

The coming of the Romans in about 43AD would have led to a few changes, but for the common person it was probably just a case of having to work a bit harder to pay the extra taxes. Nempnett might have become a Roman estate, a new lord taking over the working unit already established in the Iron Age, but with the new Roman leader living in a fancy south-facing villa. This estate might have provided food for those mining in the Mendips, as well as for the local population. To ease transportation a new road was built, to the villa near or at the local Holy site at the church. A new set of fields may have been laid out too, around the area we today call Pixey Hall, regimented fields with straightish boundaries running up and down the steep slopes there. The temple at Pagan's Hill near Chew Stoke would have been visited by the upper echelons of society for big gatherings and major festivals.

When the Romans left around 410 the local subsistence economy would have continued, the gentry now being the indigenous British or Welsh until in the 7th century the English took political control. This period marked the beginning of land ownership and the dominating role of manors in the countryside. The Nempnett estate continued to be a viable unit, with arable crops on the higher flat land in the north, seasonal grazing on Felton Common, hay meadows near the river, fish and birds from the river and wetlands, and a ready supply of wood for fuel and timber for building from the forested lands on the slopes. By 1200 the single Nempnett estate had been split up, replaced by two or more manors.

Some time between 800 and 1000 the first church would have been established, a wooden structure on the existing holy site on the east of the estate at the flat piece of land with a fine view. Most likely this was the act of a local lord, keen to establish his social and religious credentials by establishing his local church.

In 1066 the Normans arrived, and, amongst other things, replaced the gentry and took the census of land we now call the Domesday Book. Although Nempnett does not appear therein, it seems clear now that much of the northern part of the parish was by then settled, in the form of a series of dispersed farmsteads and hamlets. The main manor was Regilbury, then called Ragiol, with probably a small number of other manors also holding some lands in the parish.

Between 1000 and 1200 the church was rebuilt in stone, and a formal, carefully demarcated, ecclesiastical parish was established. The general extent of this new parish would have been based on the ancient boundaries marked by barrows and superstition. It would also have been defined with great precision, every field definitely allocated to one parish or another, every kink in the boundary carefully documented, since this allocation was the basis of the payment of tithes, the economic basis for the church. What now appear strange arrangements, like the inclusion of Butcombe Mill in the parish of Nempnett, and the land around Henmarsh Farm being part of Winford parish, would at the time have had perfectly sensibly explanations. Probably boundaries were based on ownership, with all the land of a particular farming unit being put in a single parish. And once established these boundaries would have been carefully guarded and preserved. It was only when the parish had changed to a largely civil administrative function that it made more sense to have compact parishes, and it was this shift that prompted the "tidying up" of the parish boundaries at the end of the 19th century (see Figure 3).

The period 850-1200 was marked by a major change in most parts of the countryside, the development of villages, but this passed Nempnett by, and the ancient pattern of dispersed hamlets and farms remained unchanged. In other parishes completely new planned villages were often started, probably at the behest of enterprising lords of the manor, but possibly by the local populace with the agreement of their lord, for example as appears to have happened at Burrington.[2] In other places villages grew more organically, through the merging of adjacent hamlets on suitable sites. That neither of these processes led to a village of Nempnett developing is probably down to two factors, manorial ownership and topography.

From the sketchy details available it seems likely that the pattern of manorial ownership in Nempnett was complex over this period, with various manors having holdings dotted around the parish, so that it would have been a complicated business to set up a new village here. Later, when a large section of the parish came under the control of Flaxley Abbey, Nempnett was probably a small and unimportant outlying part of an estate which had little in the way of spare funds anyway. The very hilly nature of the terrain, the location of the church and the lack of a large central manor house meant there was no "natural focus" around which a new village might grow organically. The relatively high terrain and lack of level areas may also have meant that Nempnett was less dependent on arable crops than its neighbours, and, as it seems that a heavy dependence on arable crops may have favoured the development of villages, this pressure may have been absent here.[3] Whatever the reasons, villages of the pretty-houses-round-the-duck-pond type never quite made it to Nempnett. Rather what seems to have happened in this period was the continued clearance of the wooded slopes in the south of the parish to be populated by scattered farms and hamlets, so that by, say, 1300 the pattern of settlement was much as it was today.

Like most parts of the English countryside there is a rich and complex story underlying the local landscape. Nempnett Thurbwell has a very ancient landscape, and the very rapid and profound changes of the 20th century have largely passed the parish by, at least compared to most neighbouring areas. That sense that when you visit Nempnett it is somehow "lost in time" has a great deal of truth in it. Nempnett today contains many traces from these early days; the pattern of lanes, the layout of the fields, the fact there is no central village, the location of the church on its own on the eastern boundary of the parish, all these aspects of the landscape may date back many hundreds, perhaps thousands, of years, reflecting a long complex pattern of events. This book has tried to illuminate some of the history of the parish, but there are many things we still do not know, and many puzzles to uncover still.

Appendix: Field-names

This appendix presents an analysis of the field-names recorded in the Tithe Map and Apportionment of 1841. Where earlier references have been found with significantly different spellings further details are given. The emphasis is on the first component or components of the name, that is to say the qualifier or specific, so that, for example, Brier Paddock is discussed under "Brier". The names are ordered alphabetically by the qualifier, with very similar names grouped together. Names which are self-explanatory (e.g. Six Acres) are not discussed, nor are fields named after places discussed in Chapter 4 (e.g. Regilbury Ground).

Following the name(s) is a reference to the location or locations of the field(s) as shown in Figures 49-53; for example SE/A2 means that the field in question is to be found in grid A2 of the South East map (Figure 53). With most entries are one or more sets of initials which note the main sources used in the derivation of the explanation. These are:

AM – Alan Mawer (1924) *The Chief Elements used in English Place-Names*. Part 2 of *Introduction to the Survey of English Place-names*, (Eds. A Mawer and F M Stenton) Cambridge University Press.

JF - John Field (1989) *English Field-Names*, Alan Sutton, Gloucestershire.

MG – Margaret Gelling (1984) *Place-names in the Landscape*, Pheonix, London.

OC – O G S Crawford (1924) Place-names and archaeology, in Mawer and Stenton (1924) *op. cit.*

PC - Paul Cavill (2003) personal communication.

RER - Ruth Richardson (2003) personnal communication.

The explanations given below are those judged the most probable, based on the location of the field and what is known about its history; in many cases there may be other reasons, in particular that personal names are the reason for the naming. The abbreviations OE and ME refer to Old English and Middle English.

The Allsaints. SE/A2. An unusual name because of the use of "The" which suggests something uncommon and precise. It is far removed from Nempnett Church, and from other known churches such as Butcombe, but it is likely that there was an "All Saints dedication" possibly from an individual rather than a church. One of the most puzzling names in the parish. PC.

Angle Hill. SW/C2. An L-shaped field from ME *angle*, here on a hill. JF.

Ashills Wood, **Ashills Paddock**. EC/B4, B3. After the Ash tree. JF.

Barn Close, **Barns Paddock**, **Barn Ground**. N/B2, N/C1, SE/A3. Land by or containing a barn, or similar farm building. JF.

Barrow Mead. EC/B2. Probably from OE *beorg* meaning hill or rocky mound, which in this part of England was generally used to denote an artificial hill, a barrow in the archaeological sense. Hence "meadow by a tumulus". PC, JF. There is no known barrow near these fields.

Bathfield. N/B3. Land by a pond (OE *bæð*). JF.

Bean Close, Bean Croft. SE/C2, B2. "Land on which beans were grown". JF.

Bedlam Acre, Great Bedlam Acre. WC/B1. An intriguing name, since bedlam is usually associated with houses for the insane and/or their inmates or a site where discharged patients could beg or were living. JF. There is no apparent record of such a house or site by these fields.

Bitterns Nest, Big Bitterns Nest. SE/B4. From the bird bittern.

Bosmead, Bosmead Hill, Bosmead Paddock. WC/C3. Probably from an Old English personal name, so that Bosmead means "Bosa's meadow". MG.

Bourton Field. SW/A3. A compound of the OE *burh* and *tun*. The primary meaning of *burg* is fortified place but it was often used to refer to Roman or prehistoric defensive works, barrows and the like, so this is "a settlement or enclosure by an ancient earthwork". AM, PC. These fields lie directly around and below "Hawkridge Barrow".

Bradley Way. WC/B3. Bradley: a broad clearing, OE *brad* broad and *ley*. MG.

Brier Paddock. WC/C1. Land on which briars (eglantine) grew, OE *brær*. JF.

Brimble Croft. SE/A3. Probably from OE *bræmbel* brambles, so land where they grew.

Broadmead, Broad Close, Broadclose, Broadmead Close. N/B2, SE/B4, SW/B3. A wide piece of land. JF.

Brownes Furlong. SW/A2. Probably after a personal name. PC.

Burnell. SW/C1. Possibly from the OE *burh* (see Bourton Field) and *hyll* "hill", so meaning "hill with an ancient earthwork", or "hill of the fort". Alternatively from OE *byrgan* "burial place" and *hyll* so "hill of the burial place". MG, PC.. These fields are about 200m down slope of the oval enclosure SMR 5300 (see Chapter 2).

Burrows Batch. WC/B2. Burrow probably from OE *burh* (see Bourton Field), and batch from OE *bece, bæce* a small stream in a small valley, so "the stream by the fort/ancient earthwork". RER, MG. This field is about 300m down slope of Fairy's Toot in a small valley. But possibly from rabbits' burrows.

Bursmead. WC/B1. Probably from OE *burh* (see Bourton Field), so "the meadow by the fort/ancient earthwork". PC. This field is about 200m below the Iron Age Barrow near Bicknell Farm.

Buryfield, Buryfield Orchard, Buryfield Paddock. SE/B2,B1. Bury is usually said to be derived from the OE *burh* (see Bourton Field) meaning fort or ancient earthwork, which in the dative case is *byrig*, which has become bury. OC, PC. There are no known archaeological remains near these fields.

Bushy Leaze, Bushy Mead. EC/A4. Land covered with bushes OE *busc*. JF.

Butchers Moor. SW/B1. Probably from the name or occupation of the owner. JF.

Butcord. SE/B2. A strange name but earlier references have this as Bull Cord (SRO DD/FS Box/16/4/1 *c.* 1811, Bristol Charities 1831 p251), so this may be the bull's field, with cord as a local dialect for field.

Butlers Grove. SE/B3/4. Probably from the name or occupation of the owner. JF.

Cabby Land. SE/A2. Land where cabbages were grown?

Cakes Mead, and **Lower and Upper Cakes**. SW/C3. Possibly referring to the sticky consistency of the (clayey) soil with a tendency to cake. PC.

Calves Paddock. WC/B1. Land where calves were kept. JF.

Castle. SE/C3. As well as the modern meaning also used to refer to ruined vestiges of ancient or prehistoric buildings or defences. JF, OC. There is no known archaeological site near this field.

Chitty Hill. SW/C2. In earlier documents (SRO DD/FS Box/16/4/1 *c.* 1811, Bristol Charities 1831 p251) referred to as Chickey Hill. Possibly from where chicory was grown as a fodder crop, or from the Primitive Welsh *ced* meaning wood which is the basis for Chicklade and Chitterne in Wiltshire. PC, JF.

Cholwell. WC/B2. Probably "cold stream" from the OE *ceald* cold and *well* spring or well. PC.

Clover Ground. SE/A2, SE/B3. Land where clover was grown – an essential element of the Agrarian Revolution from the mid-17th century onwards. JF.

Clump Ground. N/B1. Usually after a clump of trees, but possibly here after the group of barrows nearby on Felton Common - see Figure 11 (p19).

Copyhold Orchard. SW/B2. Copyhold being "land held at the will of the Lord of the Manor, being authenticated by a copy of the court roll". JF

Cowleaze. N/B2. Pasture or meadow land (leaze from OE *læs*) used for cows. JF.

Crab Orchard. SE/B3. Land near or growing crab-apple trees. JF.

Crow Close. SW/A3 Land frequented by crows. JF.

Cucko, Cucko Orchard. SE/A1. Alluding in some way to the cuckoo. JF.

Culnam, Great and **Little Culnam**. SW/A3. Culham may come from OE *Cula's hamm*, where Cula is a personal name and *hamm* is land by a river. MG.

Flat Acre. SE/C3. Either level ground or land enclosed from a common field. JF

Footbury. WC/B2. From foot as in "at the foot of" and OE *burh* (see Bourton Field) so "downslope from the fort/ancient earthwork". Possibly here downhill from Regilbury. RER.

Furlong, Furlong Batch, Lower Furlong. WC/B1, WC/B2, SE/C4. Furlong often denotes a close formerly part of an open field system. JF.

Goose Furlong. N/A3. Land on which geese were pastured. JF.

Granary. EC/A4. Most likely here after a granary building.

Green Acre, Green Close. EC/A4. A notably green piece of land. JF

Harts Paddock. SW/B3. After wild deer, or a personal name.

Hawcroft, Hawcroft Orchard. SW/B3. Probably from OE *haga*, then ME *haw* meaning enclosure. PC.

Hawkridge, Great Hawkyard. SW/B3, SE/C1. Alluding to the hawk, where it was seen or possibly flown. JF.

Haymead. SW/B2. Land on which grass was grown for hay. JF.

Holland Orchard (also Holland Farm). SE/A1. Probably from OE *hoh* meaning heel or hill spur, so land by a hill spur. RER, MG.

Home Close, Field, Ground or Paddock. Various. Land near the farmhouse. JF.

Hooks Hill. WC/B3. Earlier documents (SRO DD/FS Box/16/4/1 *c*. 1811, Bristol Charities 1831 p251) have this as Rooks Hill so Hooks may be a misspelling and the original meaning is land on which rooks nested or fed. JF.

Hoopers. SW/C2. Probably from the name or occupation of the owner (a hooper being a maker of hoops). RER.

Howcroft. SE/B2. Possibly from OE *hoh* hill spur [*cf.* Howgrove]. MG, RER.

Innicks. SW/C2, SW/C1. Part of an open field system temporarily enclosed. JF.

Knowle. SW/A2. From the OE *cnoll* meaning hill. MG.

Land Croft. SW/C3. Land is sometimes used in a specialised sense (as a qualifier) to denote enclosed areas of an open field system. JF, MG.

Langmead. WC/B1. From OE *lang* meaning long, so a long meadow. JF.

Lank Yard, also **Square** and **Lower Lank Yard**. SE/B3-4. Possibly lank meaning thin, referring to the soil or shape.

Legs. WC/C2. Land shaped like the framework of a stack (of corn/hay). JF.

Limekiln Ground. N/B2. Land on which lime was dug or burnt. JF.

Limesherd. SW/C2. Possibly a clearing (OE *sceard*) amongst lime trees. JF.

Long Croft, Long Ground, Long Mead, **Longlands** etc. various. Long referring to shape, maybe a variant of OE *lang* long. JF.

Mawleaze. WC/B4. Possibly from the bird maw – a mew or gull.

Morleys: Further, Lower and Under. SE/B3. A clearing in woodland. PC, MG.

Mould Riding. SW/C2-3. Riding often a clearing, mould possibly from OE *molda* meaning top of the head, or a hill. RER.

Naphill, and the **Napsticks** – Lower Middle and Upper. SE/C3-2. The Napsticks are Nap Stile in 1811 (SRO DD/FS Box/16/4/1) and Nap Hill in 1831 (Bristol Charities 1831, p512). Nap from the OE *cnæpp* meaning a short, sharp ascent, so Naphill a steep hill. Stile from OE *stigel* , "a steep ascent, or path up a steep hill" so Nap Stile a double emphasis of steepness. PC.

Nut Mead. WC/B2. Land with nut trees. JF.

Oakley. WC/B1. A clearing in woodland of oaks. MG.

Oxleaze. WC/C4, N/B3, SE/B4. Pasture land (leaze from OE *læs)* used for oxen. JF.

Phoenix Orchard. WC/B4. A wonderful name but an earlier spelling is Pennox in 1770 (SRO DD/S/WH No16) so probably from OE *pennuc*, ME *pennok*, *pinnok* meaning "a small pen", common in West Country field-names. PC.

Pit Mead. N/B3. Land by or near a pit or quarry. JF. Here possibly a quarry for strontia in the neighbouring field Whitstone Hill (see Chapter 4).

Plaisters. EC/C4. Sports place (OE *pleg-stow*) although sometimes a more serious meeting place. JF.

Poor Close, Poor Ground and Poor Tyning. Various. Probably the quality of the soil. JF.

Port Mantle and **Great Port Mantle**. SE/C3. A very unusual name. "Possibly a corruption of the French word portmanteau, a rectangular case for carrying clothes, the significance being the field having a 'folded' [sloping] appearance". PC. Alternatively may be linked in some way to Roman settlement, especially a Roman road or portway. RER.

Pound Paddock. SE/B3. After the nearby parish pound.

Rag and **Rag Orchard**. SW/C3. Rag – land on which rough stone was found. Possibly from Rug (see below). JF.

Reding Paddock. WC/A1. Probably from the red soil colour, possibly a variant of Ridings.

Ridings, **South Ridings** and **Ridings Paddock**. SE/C2, EC/B4. Ridings from OE *ryding* meaning a clearing in woodland or land taken into cultivation from waste. JF.

Rings Paddock. WC/B1. Possibly relating to prehistoric circular enclosures, from the OE *hring* meaning ring, although there are no known features nearby. See Trendle Mead which is nearby. JF, RER.

Rug Paddock, **Rugmoor**. SW/C3-4. Possibly land covered with large stones, but more likely from OE *ruh* meaning rough or uncultivated. JF, PC.

Rushey Mead. WC/B3. Land covered with rushes. JF.

Shutwells. N/A-B4. Shut usually alludes to part of an old common arable field from OE *sceat* for nook, corner or point (as used in fields), and well to a spring OE *wella*. JF.

Sideland. various. Land alongside another piece of land or a stream. JF.

Slade Piece. EC/A3. Land in a marshy valley, OE *slæd* low flat valley, used in different ways in dialect often for marshy land. JF, AM.

Splotts. SW/B3. Probably from ME *splot* a piece of land. JF

Sprodes Paddock. WC/B2. Probably from a personal name. PC

Stable Field, Great and Little. EC/A4. Land adjoining or with a stable. JF.

Stackridge. SW/B2. Possibly from stack, land containing stack of corn or hay, plus ridge, or, more likely, from OE *staca*, stake, so "ridge of land with boundary stakes" or similar. JF.

Stews. SE/A4. Land containing fish ponds or tanks, ME *stewe*. JF.

Summerleaze. N/A4. Land used in the summer. JF.

Swamp Paddock. WC/B1. Boggy land. JF.

Swans Nest. SW/A2. Land on or near which swans were found. JF.

Swilly Mead. WC/B-C3. Probably from OE *swile* as "muddy, messy land". PC.

Tee Paddock. WC/C1. T-shaped piece of land. JF

The Tent. WC/B3. Unusual because of the use of "The". The name Tenter Field is usually a field where cloth is stretched, from ME *teyntour* a cloth stretching-frame, but that seems unlikely here. Possibly derived, perhaps by misspelling, from OE *tot* a look-out place and here specifically referring to the Fairy's Toot barrow which is in this field (see Chapter 3). PC.

Thatchers Moor. SW/B2. Probably from the name or occupation of the owner. JF.

Three Corner Paddock. N/B4. Describing the triangular shape. JF.

Trendle Mead. WC/B2. Probably from the OE *trendel* meaning "a round thing, a circular structure" so possibly relating to prehistoric circular enclosures, although there are no known features nearby. See Rings Paddock which is nearby. PC

Twinyard, and **Great** and **Little Twinyards**. EC/A1&B2. Twin probably meaning between, here between the streams. RER.

Voathays. SE/B1. Very unusual. Possibly a surname or a dialect version of wood hays, a fenced enclosure by a wood. PC

Well Close, **Ground and Paddock**. N/B3, SE/B1. Land by a well or spring. JF

Wetgars. SW/B-C3. Probably from wet and grass (OE *gærs*), so a damp meadow.

Wheat Croft, **Wheat Ground**. SE/B2, SW/C3. Land on which wheat grew well. JF.

Whitstone Hill. N/B3. White stone, probably because strontia was mined nearby.

Whole Lands. SW/B2. Probably from OE *hoh* for heel, hill spur or OE *hol* hollow, or possibly in the sense of "wholesome". RER.

Woodyhern. WC/C1. Woody plus hern a nook or corner of land (OE *hyrne*). JF.

Yewlands. SE/B4. Usually relating to the yew tree, but unlikely here given that these fields are so close to the River Yeo. Perhaps a misspelling of Newlands, the name of adjacent fields, or Yeo lands.

References and Notes

Abbreviations used in this section:

Aston and Iles (1975): Aston Michael and Rob Iles (Eds) *The Archaeology of Avon: A Review from the Neolithic to the Middle Ages*
BRO: Bristol Record Office (followed by reference number).
GRO: Gloucester Record Office (followed by reference number).
PRO: Public Record Office (followed by reference number).
PUBSS: Proceedings of the University of Bristol Speleological Society
SANHS: Somerset Archaeological and Natural History Society Proceedings
SDNQ: Somerset & Dorset Notes & Queries
SRO: Somerset Record Office (followed by reference number).

CHAPTER 1: INTRODUCTION

Notes for Chapter 1:

1. Aston M, Medieval Settlements in Avon, in Aston and Iles (1975), p99.
2. Derived from aerial photographs held by the English Heritage's National Monuments Record in Swindon, Sorties 3G/TUD/UK for 4 December 1946, frames 4239, 3250, 3251, 4257 and 4255 and sortie CPE/UK/1869 for 14 January 1946 frames 5077, 5129 and 5131. The composite photograph shown in Figure 5 was made by the author.

CHAPTER 2: PREHISTORIC AND ROMAN TIMES

The Butcombe excavations are discussed in:

Fowler P J, 1968, Excavation of a Romano-British Settlement at Row of Ashes Farm, Butcombe, 1966-1967, *PUBSS*, 11, 209-236.

Fowler PJ, 1970, Fieldwork and Excavation in the Butcombe Area, North Somerset, Second Interim Report, 1968-9, *PUBSS*, 12,2, 169-194.

Fowler P J 1975, Continuity in the landscape? Some Local Archaeology in Wiltshire, Somerset and Gloucestershire, in P J Fowler (Ed) *Recent Work in Rural Archaeology*, Moonraker Press, Wiltshire.

Fowler P J, 1978, Pre-Medieval Fields in the Bristol Region, in *Early Land Allotment in the British Isles*, HC Bowen and PJ Fowler (Eds), British Archaeological Report No. 48.

See also:

Haverfield F J, 1906, Roman Somerset, *Victoria History of Somerset*, Vol 1.

Neale F, 1970, The site of the Roman villa at Hayatt, Somerset, *PUBSS*, 12,2, 195-202.

Tratman E K, 1960, The rediscovery of the Roman villa at Lye Hole, Somerset, *PUBSS*, 9,1, 33-35.

The Chew Valley Lake excavations are reported in full in:

Rahtz P A and E Greenfield, 1977, *Excavations at Chew Valley Lake*, Somerset, HMSO, London.

The Pagan's Hill temple is discussed in:

Rahtz P and L Watts, 1989, Pagans Hill revisited, *Archaeological Journal*, 146, 330-371.

For barrows and the Iron and Bronze Ages see:

Grinsell Leslie 1966 *Prehistoric Sites in the Mendip, South Cotswold and Bristol Region*, Bristol Archaeological Research Group

Grinsell Leslie, 1971, Somerset Barrows, Part II, *SANHS*, Vol 115, 45-137

OSAR – Ordnance Survey Archaeological Reports, available at Taunton Local Studies Library.

Rahtz P A and M H Rahtz, 1958, T.40: Barrow and Windmill at Butcombe, North Somerset, *PUBSS*, 8,2,89-97.

SMR: The Sites and Monuments Record held in the Planning Offices at Bath and North East Somerset, Trim Street, Bath.

Tratman E K, 1925, Field Work, *PUBSS*, 2,3,274-289.

Tratman E K, 1938, Field Work, *PUBSS*, 5,1, 80-86.

Important general references on North Somerset (Avon) are:

Bird S, 1976, Roman Avon, Ch 5 in Aston and Iles (1975):

Burrow I, 1976, Hillforts and the Iron Age, Ch 4 in Aston and Iles (1975):

Darvill T, 1976, Neolithic Avon, Ch 2 in Aston and Iles (1975):

Dobson D P, 1931 *The Archaeology of Somerset*, Methuen.

Grinsell L, 1976, Bronze Age Settlement and Burial Ritual, Ch 3 in Aston
and Iles (1975):
Hebditch M and L Grinsell, 1968, *Roman Sites in the Mendip, Cotswold, Wye
Valley and Bristol Region*, Bristol Archaeological Research Guide Field
Guide No 2.

An excellent text on Aerial Photography and Archaeology is:

Wilson D R, 2000, *Air Photo Interpretation for Archaeologists*, Tempus, Stroud.

On boundaries see:

Fowler P J and I Blackwell, 1998, The *Land of Lettice Sweetapple; An English
Countryside Explored*, Tempus, Stroud.
Rackham O, 1986, *The History of the Countryside*, Pheonix Grant, London.
Winchester A, 1990, *Discovering Parish Boundaries*, Shire Publications.

Notes for Chapter 2:

1. ff58 in Skinner Rev J, 1822, Diary, British Library MSS 28793-5, 33633-
   730.
2. I am grateful to Vince Russett for this information.
3. I am grateful to Peter Fowler for this information.
4. The aerial photographs are from Sortie CPE/UK/1869, frames 3250-
   3251.
5. see Rackham (1986), pp19 and 21.

CHAPTER 3: FAIRY'S TOOT

The main primary references on Fairy's Toot are:

Bere Rev Thomas, 1789a, Letter to *Bath Chronicle*. [Fully quoted in Bulleid
(1941, p60-1).]
Bere Rev Thomas 1789b *Gentleman's Magazine*, Vol 59, Part 1, 392-393.
Bere Rev Thomas, 1792 *Gentleman's Magazine*, Vol 62, Part 2, 1082-1084 and
1181-1183.
Bulleid A, 1941 "Notes on Some Chambered Long Barrows in N
Somerset", *SANHS*, 87, 56-71.
Dobson D P, 1931 *The Archaeology of Somerset*, Methuen.
Rutter J, 1827 *Delineations of Somersetshire*.
Skinner Rev J, 1822, Diary, British Library MSS 28793-5, 33633-730.
Tumboracos, 1789 *Gentleman's Magazine*, Vol 59, Part 2, 605-606.

For more on Stoney Littleton see:

Colt Hoare R, 1821, "An account of a stone barrow in the parish of
Wellow, at Stoney Littleton in the County of Somerset, which was

204

opened and investigated in the month of May 1816", *Archaeologica*, Vol 19, 43-48.

Donovan D T, 1977, Stoney Littleton Long Barrow, *Antiquity*, Vol 51, 236-237.

Thomas A, 2003, Stoney Littleton long barrow: archaeological investigations and observations 1999-200, *SANHS*, 146, 11-16.

For Cotswold-Severn Tombs in general see:

Clifford E M and Daniel G, 1940, "The Rodmartin and Avening Portholes", *Proceedings Prehistory Society,* 6, 133-165.

Corcoran J X V P, 1969, "The Cotswold-Severn Group", Chs 2 and 3, 13-106, in *Megalithic Enquiries in the West of Britain*, Ed T G E Powell.

Daniel G E, 1950, *The Prehistoric Chamber Tombs of England and Wales*, Cambridge.

Darvill T, 1976, Neolithic Avon, Ch 2 in Aston and Iles (1975).

Darvill T, 1982, *The Megalithic Chambered Tombs of the Cotswold-Severn Region*, Vorda.

Powell T G E, (Ed) 1969, *Megalithic Enquiries in the West of Britain*, Liverpool University Press.

Saville A, 1990, *Hazleton North*, English Heritage Archaeological Report No 13.

Scarth Rev HM, 1858, "Remarks on Ancient Chambered Tombs", *SANHS*, Vol 8, 35-62.

Thurnam J, 1869, "On ancient British barrows, especially those of Wiltshire and the adjoining counties, Part I, Long Barrows", *Archaelogica*, Vol 42, 161-244.

Notes for Chapter 3:

1. Dobson D P, 1931 *The Archaeology of Somerset*, Methuen, p52.
2. Corcoran (1969), p27.
3. Skinner (1822), ff 143.
4. Samuel S , 1821, *Memoirs Historical and Topographical of Bristol and its Neighbourhood* 107-8.
5. Saville (1990), p265.
6. Corcoran (1976), p78.
7. Powell (1976), p 268.
8. Saville (1990), p257.
9. Saville (1990), p266.
10. Skinner (1820), ff58.
11. Grinsell (1971), p75.
12. Scarth (1858), p56.
13. Scarth (1858), p56.
14. Elton M, 1994, *Annals of the Elton Family, Bristol Merchants and Somerset Landowners*, Alan Sutton, p113
15. Clifford and Daniel (1940), p149.
16. Grinsell, (1971), p 75.
17. Bulleid (1941), p 64.
18. Grinsell (1971), p76.

19. Skinner (1820), ff 35.
20. Skinner (1820), ff 34.
21. Skinner (1822), ff 143.
22. Skinner (1822), ff 143.
23. Skinner (1822), ff 143.
24. Dobson (1931), p52.
25. Collinson John, 1791, *The History and Antiquities of the County of Somerset*, vol 2, p318-9.
26. Grinsell (1971), p76.
27. Skinner (1820), ff58.

CHAPTER 4: PLACE-NAMES

I was greatly helped in the writing of this chapter by Dr Paul Cavill Research Fellow, English Place-Name Society, School of English, University of Nottingham. The main references on place-names used here are:

Costen M, 1979, "Place name evidence in South Avon", *Avon Past*, 1, 13-17.
Ekwall E, 1947, *The Concise Oxford Dictionary of English Place Names*,
Gelling M, 1984, *Place Names in the Landscape,* Phoenix Press, London.
Mawer A and FM Stenton (Eds), 1924, *Introduction to the Survey of English Place Names,* 2 parts, Cambridge University Press.
Watts V (Ed), 2004, *Cambridge Dictionary of English Place-names*, Cambridge University Press.

Notes for Chapter 4:

1. SRO DD/S/WH 199.
2. SRO DD/WY.
3. Finn W R and P Wheatley, 1967, Somerset, Chapter 3 in Darby H C and R W Finn (Eds), 1967, *The Domesday Geography of South West England,* Cambridge University Press, p145.
4. Kings Court Rolls, 1931, Vol V, p188.
5. Crawley-Boevey, A W, 1887, *The Cartulary and Historical Notes of the Cistercian Abbey of Flaxley Abbey*, pp67, 78, 115 and 124.
6. *The Calendar of the Manuscripts of the Dean and Chapter of Wells* 1907, Vol 1, p485.
7. The slopes were derived digitally using Geographical Information Systems software.
8. SRS (Somerset Records Society), Vol 11, 1897, p 9.
9. Green E, 1892, *Feet of Fines for the County of Somerset, Richard I to Edward I, 1196-1307*, p107.
10. *The Calendar of the Manuscripts of the Dean and Chapter of Wells*, 7, p485.
11. Crawley-Boevey (1887), pp 74 and 113.

12. Rutter J, 1827 *Delineations of Somersetshire*, p 123.
13. BRO 4549(28).
14. SRO DD/S/WH 223 and 224.
15. Green (1892), p107
16. SRO DD/HB6.
17. SRO DD/S/WH180 No 7, and SRO DD/S/WH 224.
18. SRO DD/S/WH 224.
19. Crawley-Boevey 1887, p67.
20. Skinner MS 33673, August 21 1822 ff144.
21. DD/S/WH 180 Nos 7 & 100.
22. D.K.T. (probably David Kemeys Tynte), 1914, Strontia in Somerset, *SDNQ*, Vol 15, p287.
23. SRO DD/S/WH 199.
24. DD/S/WH 180 No 6, DD/FS Box 16/4/1.
25. SRO DD/S/WH 111.
26. for example DD/S/WH 180 No 1, DD/FS Box 16/4/1.
27. Costen (1979), p 13.
28. Costen (1979), p 13.

CHAPTER 5: FIELD-NAMES

I was greatly helped in the writing of this chapter by Dr Paul Cavill Research Fellow, English Place-Name Society, School of English, University of Nottingham. The main references on field-systems used here are:

Aston M, 1985, *Interpreting the Landscape: Landscape Archaeology and Local History*, Routledge, London.
Aston M, 1988, Land Use and Field Systems, Ch5 in *Aspects of the Medieval Landscape of Somerset*, Ed M Aston, Bridgewater.
Avon Historic Landscape Characterisation, 1995-98, unpublished ms available from Bath & NE Somerset Council, Planning Dept.
Iles R, 1976, The Medieval Rural Landscape, Ch 9 in Aston and Iles (1975).
Taylor Christopher, 1975, *Fields in the English Landscape*, London.

For field-names see especially:

Field John, 1989, *English Field Names*, A Dictionary, Alan Sutton Gloucester.

Notes for Chapter 5:

1. Rackham O, 1986, *The History of the Countryside*, Pheonix Grant, London.
2. Iles R (1976), p 118-9.
3. Aston 1985, p122 – see also Fowler 1968, 1970 [full references given in Chapter 2 notes] for examples in Butcombe parish.

4. Air Photo reference 3G/TUD/UK/15/25 Frame 5076.
5. Aston (1988), p 91.
6. Iles 1976, p 115.
7. SRO DD/X/HLL.
8. Aston (1988), p 84.
9. Aston (1988), p 84 and Iles 1967, p117.
10. SRO DD/X/HLL.
11. SRO DD/X/HLL.
12. see Aston (1985), ch 9.

CHAPTER 6: THE MANOR OF REGILBURY 1086-1536

For The Domesday Book see:

Bates Rev E H, 1899, The five-hide-unit in the Somerset Domesday, *SANHS*, 49, 51-107.

Eyton R W, 1880, *Domesday Studies: An Analysis and Digest of the Somerset Survey*, 2 vols, London.

Finn W R and P Wheatley, 1967, Somerset, Chapter 3 in Darby H C and R W Finn (Eds), 1967, *The Domesday Geography of South West England*, Cambridge University Press.

Morland S C, 1954-5, Some Domesday Manors, *SANHS*, 99/100, 38-48.

Morland S C, 1964, Further notes on Somerset Domesday, *SANHS*, 108, 94-98.

Morland S C, 1981, Maps illustrating Somerset as in the Domesday Book, unpublished ms and maps, Taunton Local Studies Library.

Thorn C and F Thorn, 1980, *Domesday Book: Somerset*, Phillimore, Chichester.

For Serlo de Burci and the Martin Family see:

Lyte, Sir Henry C Maxwell, 1919, Burci, Falaise and Martin, *SANHS*, 65, 1-27.

Watson W, 1906, *House of Martin, ,* Exeter: William Pollard.

On Flaxley Abbey see:

Crawley-Boevey, A W, 1887, *The Cartulary and Historical Notes of the Cistercian Abbey of Flaxley Abbey*.

Crawley-Boevey, Sir F H, 1914, *Notes of the History of Flaxley Abbey*, pamphlet, Gloucester Local Studies Library.

Watkins B, 1985, *The Story of Flaxley Abbey*, Alan Sutton Publishing.

Notes for Chapter 6:

1. Eyton (1880), p147.
2. Neale F in Fowler PJ, 1970, Fieldwork and Excavation in the Butcombe

Area, North Somerset, 1968-9, *PUBSS*, 12,2, 169-194

3.   Watkins (1985), p226.
4.   Lyte (1919), p11.
5.   Crawley-Boevey (1887), pp65-6, 190-2.
6.   Watkins (1985), p35.
7.   Watkins (1985), p257.
8.   Page (1907), p94, Crawley-Boevey (1887), pp65-6.
9.   Crawley-Boevey (1887), pp66-7.
10. Crawley-Boevey (1887), pp67-8, Watkins (1985), p214.
11. Kings Court Rolls, (1931), p188.
12. Feudal Aids, 1899, *Inquisitions and Assessments relating to Feudal Aids and other Anlagous Documents preserved in the Public Record Office 1284-143*, London HMSO, Vol 4, p324.
13. BRO 4549(28).
14. Feudal Aids (1899), Vol 4, pp 304, 348 and 381, Dickinson F H, 1889, *Kirby's Quest for Somerset,* Somerset Records Society.

CHAPTER 7:   THE MANOR OF REGILBURY 1537-1860

General references for this period include:

Baber V, 2003, The Baber Family Tree, at www.baberfamilytree.org
Balmer N, 2000, article on Edward Baber, at www.baberfamilytree.org
Dunning R, 2002, *Somerset Families*, Somerset Books, Taunton.
Hester P W, 1981, *The History of Parliament, The House of Commons* 1558-1603.
Kemeys-Tynte, St D, 1919, Regilbury, Somerset, *SDNQ*, Vol XVI, Pt CXXIV, 121-124.
Transactions of the Somerset Masters Lodge (1963, 87-89).
Watkins B, 1985, *The Story of Flaxley Abbey*, Alan Sutton Publishing.

Notes for Chapter 7:

1.   GRO D18/186.
2.   PRO, PROB 11/60 24Langley.
3.   PRO, PROB 11/60 24Langley.
4.   SDNQ, Vol 4, 1895, p151.
5.   Wade W. Cecil 1898 *The Symbolisms of Heraldry or A Treatise on the Meanings and Derivations of Armorial Bearings*, London.
6.   PRO PROB11/61, 8 Bakon.
7.   BRO AC/02/9.
8.   Gallannaugh R, 2001, illustrations in *The Book of Regil* (Ed) M Oliphant, GraphicType Ltd, Chew Stoke
9.   SRO DD/S/WH 223a and 229.
10. Skinner (1832), ff144 - see Chapter 3 notes for full reference.

CHAPTER 8: THE GEOGRAPHY OF THE MANOR OF REGILBURY 1730

Note for Chapter 8:

1. Gelling Margaret, 1984, *Place-Names in the Landscape*, Phoenix Press, London, pp100-111.

CHAPTER 9: OTHER MANORS

Important general references are:

Collinson John, 1791, *The History and Antiquities of the County of Somerset*
Dickinson F H, 1889, *Kirby's Quest for Somerset*, Somerset Records Society.
Feudal Aids, 1899, *Inquisitions and Assessments relating to Feudal Aids and other Anlagous Documents preserved in the Public Record Office 1284-143*, London HMSO.
Green E, 1892, *Feet of Fines for the County of Somerset, Richard I to Edward I, 1196-1307.*
Neale F, 1970, "Early History" section in Fowler PJ, 1970, Fieldwork and Excavation in the Butcombe Area, North Somerset, Second Interim Report, 1968-9, *PUBSS*, 12,2, 169-194.
Rutter J, 1827, *Delineations of Somersetshire.*

Notes for Chapter 9:

1. see Collinson (1791), Vol 2, p314 and Rutter (1829), p123.
2. Wade W. Cecil, 1898, *The Symbolisms of Heraldry or A Treatise on the Meanings and Derivations of Armorial Bearings*, London.
3. Collinson has as the original reference "Rot. Pip. 24 Hen. II".
4. SRS (Somerset Records Society) 1897, Volume 11, *Rolls of the Itinerant Justices (Somerset Pleas)* edited by C Chadwyck-Healey SRS, 1897, pp9-10)
5. Green (1892), p107.
6. *Calendar of the Manuscripts of the Dean and Chapter of Wells* (1907), Vol 1, p485.
7. BRO 4549(28).
8. Collinson (1791), Vol 2, pp313-4, Yvery, 1742, , *Genealogical History of the House of Yvery Vol 1* p83.
9. SRO T/PH/vch 86.
10. PRO C/1/1185/56-58.
11. Rutter (1829), p123 and Collinson (1791), Vol 2, p314.
12. Neale (1970), p175.
13. PRO C12/2147/5.
14. Collinson (1791) Vol 2, p315, and Page W (Ed), 1907, *Victoria County*

History of Gloucestershire, Vol 2, p160.

15. SRO DD/QK 51.
16. SRO DD/BRC/14 & 17.
17. SRO DD/X/HLL.
18. SRO DD/S/ST 19.1.
19. see Feudal Aids (1899), Vol 1, pp 324, 327 and 381, Dickenson, (1889).
20. Wade E F, 1880, Notes on the family of Prowse, of Compton Bishop, Co. Somerset, *Miscellanea Genealogica et Heraldica*, pp167-8.
21. SRO DD/S/WH 111.
22. SRO DD/WY.
23. Collinson (1791), p319, and Eyton R W, 1880, *Domesday Studies: An Analysis and Digest of the Somerset Survey*, 2 vols, London 1880, Vol 1, p148.
24. Thorn C and F Thorn, 1980, *Domesday Book: Somerset*, Phillimore, Chichester, p366.
25. Morland S C, 1981, Maps illustrating Somerset as in the Domesday Book, unpublished ms and maps, Taunton Local Studies Library.
26. Green (1892), p307.
27. Crawley-Boevey, A W, 1887, *The Cartulary and Historical Notes of the Cistercian Abbey of Flaxley Abbey*, pp185-9.

CHAPTER 10: AN OVERVIEW

Notes for Chapter 10:

1. This chapter is based on section three of the excellent *The Land of Lettice Sweetapple* by P Fowler and I Blackwell, 1998, Tempus.
2. Nick Corcos, 2002, Bourne and Burrington: a Burnantun estate?, *SANHS*, 144, 117-138.
3. C Lewis, P Mitchell-Fox and C Dyer, 1997, *Village, Hamlet and Field*, Manchester University Press.

Index